*Invisible Friends*

# Invisible Friends

*The Correspondence of*
*Elizabeth Barrett Barrett*
*and*
*Benjamin Robert Haydon*
*1842–1845*

*edited by*

*Willard Bissell Pope*

*Harvard University Press*
*Cambridge, Massachusetts*
*1972*

Publication of this book has been aided by a grant from the
Hyder Edward Rollins Fund

To E. R. P.

# Contents

# Illustrations

# Introduction

The correspondents Elizabeth Barrett Barrett and Benjamin Robert Haydon are more interesting as people than as a poet and a painter. "Sonnets from the Portuguese" are no longer considered superb poetry of love, nor are Mrs. Browning's other works widely read. So it is with Haydon as an artist; his pictures are rarely sold, because few collectors or museums wish to purchase them, and the majority of the two hundred-odd oils he painted are lost. As people, however, they remain vibrant and interesting. The nineteenth century contains no more fascinating stories than those of the romantic elopement of the Brownings and the harrowing suicide of Haydon.

In 1842 Mary Mitford suggested that her friends Elizabeth Barrett Barrett and Benjamin Robert Haydon commence an epistolary friendship. She had known both for years, seeing them infrequently but corresponding more or less regularly, since she seldom went from Three Mile Cross, Hampshire, to London. She felt that personal meetings were unnecessary for friendship so long as letters could be exchanged.

At the time this mutually pleasant correspondence began, Elizabeth Barrett rarely left her room in her father's house at 50 Wimple Street. She had been seriously ill in her teens and in 1838 became a confirmed invalid. That year she began a two-year residence in Torquay, Devon, in the hope that sea-air would benefit her health. During the summer of 1840 her favorite brother Edward, "Bro," fifteen months her junior, drowned when his boat capsized. Because he had come to Torquay solely to visit her, she blamed herself for his death. This unreasonable sense of guilt greatly increased her physical ailments — weakness of the spine, lungs, and blood-vessels — and resulted in deep-seated hypochondria.

Miss Mitford must have introduced Haydon in glowing terms or her friend would never have consented to correspond with him. Miss Barrett's reputation as a poet, essayist, and translator was well established; she was a complete recluse, however, seeing few people except the members of her large family, her father, brothers, sisters, and cousins. Invalid that she was, she showed great energy in the sheer volume of her writing — poetry, essays, and a truly voluminous correspondence. In addition to Haydon, she wrote frequently to Sir Uvedale Price, Hugh Stuart Boyd, Richard Henry Horne, John Kenyon, Mary Mitford, and Harriet Martineau.

Soon after the correspondence with Haydon ceased, Miss Barrett, after neurotically alleging many obstacles to a meeting with Robert Browning, summoned up her courage to permit a personal call from him, the first of a series of clandestine visits which culminated in their elopement on September 19, 1846. Autocratic Edward Barrett had never subdued this brave, high-spirited woman. She was a dutiful daughter as well as a courageous wife, and always deeply regretted the fact that her father refused to see her or even to read the letters she sent him after her marriage.

In spite of many requests, Elizabeth Barrett refused to receive Haydon, though she welcomed his letters and miscellanea such as sketches, pamphlets, and a tea-urn which he lent her. Tuft-hunter that he was, his correspondence with the distinguished "Aeschylus" Barrett was well worth cultivating, and he wrote eagerly in spite of some frustration that she declined to let him call. Though faithful to his marriage vows, Haydon was habitually attracted to ladies. He made a fool of himself during his infatuation with the Hon. Mrs. Caroline Norton in 1833; he basked in Mrs. Siddons' praise for his painting "Christ's Entry into Jerusalem"; his acquaintance with attractive women, particularly peeresses like Lady Seymour and the Countess of Blessington, gave him great joy; and even an unattractive bluestocking like Miss Mitford remained an admired friend for many years.

Haydon probably never realized that Miss Barrett was far from beautiful or that, like many invalids of her time, she depended heavily on drugs, taking forty drops of laudanum, a tincture of opium, each day on doctor's orders. He knew only that she was a learned celebrity whose interesting and amusing letters to him probably would not exist had a face-to-face friendship developed.

Elizabeth Barrett Barrett was born at Coxhoe Hall, Durham, in 1806, twenty years after Haydon and six years before Robert Browning. She was the eldest of twelve children of Edward Barrett Moulton, who added the surname of Barrett when he inherited the Jamaica estates of his maternal grandfather. Like Haydon, who was dedicated to painting all his mature life, Miss Barrett from childhood on was completely devoted to poetry, reading it in several languages and practicing the writing of it with great tenacity. An intellectual prodigy, she could read Greek at the age of eight and began to write poetry when still a child. Her *Battle of Marathon,* an epic influenced by Homer in both the original and Pope's translation, so pleased her father that in 1820 he had fifty copies privately printed. He encouraged further studies in the classics, which led to Elizabeth's translation of Aeschylus' *Prometheus Bound,* eventually published in 1833.

With Wordsworth in decline, Coleridge and Scott moribund and then dying, and neither Browning nor Tennyson at his peak, the 1830's produced no great English literature. Miss Barrett deserves consideration as the leading poet of this period, with *The Seraphim and Other Poems* (1838), the first work issued under her own name, and numerous contributions to the *New Monthly Magazine.* Although she was now receiving favorable critical attention, the end of this decade marks the severe decline of her health and her consequent withdrawal from society. The isolation gave her greater opportunities to study and to continue writing, including four scholarly articles on Greek Christian poets, published in *The Athenaeum*.

When they started to exchange letters, Miss Barrett's best years lay ahead, but Haydon's were far behind. Yet, although misfortunes filled the four years until his suicide, in writing her he retained his inherent ebullience; this correspondence does not reveal the disappointments of the period, which are poignantly recorded in his diary.

Benjamin Robert Haydon was born in Plymouth in 1786, the son of a bookseller, to whom he was apprenticed. Anatomy, drawing, and the history of art consumed his interests, and even a serious illness resulting in temporary blindness and permanent extreme myopia failed to weaken his obsession to become an artist. At eighteen his father reluctantly canceled his indentures and sent him to London to study at the Royal Academy under Fuseli.

His career as a student was a series of intoxicating experiences. Fuseli was a stimulating teacher and friend; amiable patronage by Sir George Beaumont and Lord Mulgrave established lifelong contacts with wealthy and noble connoisseurs and presaged his friendship with a great number of artistic, literary, and political leaders. Enmities also resulted, for Haydon was quick to rush to the defense of and fight for his principles and beliefs. He permanently disqualified himself for membership in the Royal Academy by attacking the "organization." He also did great service to art by pugnaciously defending the Elgin Marbles against influential detractors soon after they reached England in 1808.

Until 1823, when Haydon was imprisoned for debt (three similar imprisonments followed), happy events greatly outnumbered the sad ones. His marriage in 1821 to Mary Hyman, a widow with two sons, was most felicitous; friendships with Wilkie, Wordsworth, Keats, and many others gave him great pleasure; travels in England and Scotland and especially in France—in 1814, when Napoleon was in Elba and all the looted treasures of art were in the Louvre—were stimulating and delightful; but Haydon's greatest pleasure was his establishment as a successful artist through exhibition of such paintings as "The Assassination of Dentatus," "The Judgement of Solomon," "Christ's Entry into Jerusalem," and "The Raising of Lazarus." Although the pictures were well reviewed and attracted crowds to their exhibitions, Haydon failed to sell them profitably, and the seeds of his financial troubles were sown during this period, with improvident borrowing from usurers to pay for his extravagances.

A second imprisonment for debt occurred in 1827, after his wife had borne him two sons and a daughter. Five more children completed the family but contributed more sorrow than joy, since five of the eight died in infancy. But, as Haydon frequently recorded in his diary, quoting from *All's Well That Ends Well:* "the web of our life is of a mingled yarn."

An ardent Whig, Haydon advocated parliamentary reform, and like Miss Barrett, he was elated when the Reform Bill of 1832 was passed. He was especially happy to be commissioned to paint the banquet held by leaders of the party and their friends in celebration of this victory. Not content to execute the picture just from sketches he made during the banquet, he persuaded most of those present to pose in his studio for individual portrait sketches; thus he became acquainted with such Whig leaders as Earl Grey and Lord Melbourne. He also knew leaders of the opposition like Sir Robert Peel and the Duke of Wellington, whose portrait he painted after a three-day visit at Walmer Castle. Many portraits by Haydon, such as this one of the Duke and the one of Wordsworth in the National Portrait Gallery, are considered excellent likenesses. The great canvas of the Reform Banquet, however, is a failure, as is a similar painting of the Anti-Slavery Convention of 1840. Following his procedure with "The Reform Banquet," he obtained individual sittings from the world's leading abolitionists who attended this international gathering.

Beside his career as a painter, Haydon established himself

as a lecturer, delivering talks on the fine arts in many cities and publishing them in two volumes. Throughout most of his artistic life he was a frequent contributor of letters to newspapers and magazines on controversial artistic subjects.

In 1842, about the time when he commenced his correspondence with Miss Barrett, he learned of a competition for cartoons, to be executed as frescoes for the new Houses of Parliament, replacing those destroyed by fire in 1834. Having favored active governmental support of all the graphic arts for many years, he enthusiastically endorsed the competition, learning the technique of fresco painting so that he could enter it. He was crushed, therefore, when he learned that his designs were rejected. This failure was the beginning of the end. The final blow fell in the spring of 1846, when an exhibition of his latest works failed completely, largely because of an intensely popular rival attraction exhibited by Phineas Barnum in another chamber of the Egyptian Hall: "General" Tom Thumb.

Foreseeing another arrest for debt and hoping to arouse public sympathy for his wife, on June 23, 1846, Benjamin Robert Haydon killed himself.

The existing correspondence between Haydon and Miss Barrett ends with a letter from him written more than a year before his death. Describing the termination of the correspondence, Miss Barrett wrote to Browning on the day of the suicide: "It is nearly two years since we had a correspondence of some few months—from which at last I receded, notwithstanding the individuality and spirit of his letters, & my admiration for a certain fervour & magnanimity of genius, no one could deny him. His very faults partook of that nobleness. But for a year & a half or more perhaps, I scarcely have written or heard from him—until last week when he wrote to ask for a shelter for [some of] his boxes & pictures," including his diary.* Miss Barrett was shattered by news of his

---

* *Letters of Robert Browning and Elizabeth Barrett Barrett, 1845–1846,* London, 1899, II, 264.

death and, in letters to her fiancé, brooded over the thought that a gift or loan from her might have saved his life. On Browning's advice, she wisely declined to edit the diary as Haydon had requested and returned it to Mrs. Haydon.

Grief for her epistolary friend did not deter Miss Barrett's romance. Three months after Haydon's death she married Robert Browning; they eloped to Italy for fifteen idyllic years of great literary achievement for both. Queen Victoria was urged to name her poet laureate on the death of Wordsworth in 1850, but chose instead to honor her favorite, Tennyson. Elizabeth Barrett Browning published *Poems* (including "Sonnets from the Portuguese") in 1850, *Casa Guidi Windows* in 1851, *Aurora Leigh* in 1857, and other volumes of poetry. But her health, though greatly improved after she left England, was still frail, and she died in Florence on June 29, 1861.

Documents like these letters, which reveal facets of the personalities of famous or romantic people, are useful to students and titillating to general readers, who frequently enjoy the vice of surreptitiously perusing letters not addressed to them. If one may judge from the salutations, their literary friendship was truly meaningful to both correspondents. To Miss Barrett, Haydon was "my dear kind friend." He was far more effusive, addressing her by such titles as "you Ingenious little darling invisible" and "my dearest dream & invisible intellectuality" — though, in spite of his familiarity, never using the more intimate nickname "Ba." As the correspondence progressed, more and more confidences were exchanged. Miss Barrett wrote of her poor health and, without really complaining, of her virtual imprisonment in her father's house. Haydon went even further in his confidential revelations, sending drafts of his autobiography as they were written, thus permitting her to read what no one else had seen, and, when he feared arrest for debt, entrusting her with valuables which he believed would be seized.

Although naturally he longed to meet her in person, Haydon never thought of terminating the correspondence because of

Miss Barrett's steadfast refusal to receive him. Instead he found "something so original in a couple of Geniuses corresponding, becoming acquainted, knowing each other thoroughly & yet never seeing each other, that I revelled in the Idea beyond expression."

Unfortunately the correspondence is lopsided, with ninety-four letters of Haydon to twenty-eight of Miss Barrett. Many letters obviously were lost or destroyed, but Haydon surely wrote more often than she did, for example, sending her twelve extant letters during the month of May 1843, and on two occasions writing twice on the same day. With complete candor he admitted that egotism was the basis of his pleasure in the correspondence. "I never ask what *you* are doing," he wrote, "but take it for granted what *I* am doing must be delightful to you."

Haydon therefore wrote about his contention with the Royal Academy, his career as a lecturer, his achievement in securing recognition for the Elgin Marbles, his apathetic view of Queen Victoria. He described his types of painting and the actual composition of many of his pictures; indeed he appealed to her for assistance on the historical background of "The Black Prince Entering London in Triumph" and the validity of introducing Chaucer and Gower among the crowd. He discussed many of his friends, notably Keats, in whom she seems to have been most interested. Although the first biography of Keats did not appear until 1848, his poems were still in print during the correspondence and, like her future husband, Miss Barrett was an enthusiastic Keatsian.

Haydon described his trip to France in 1814, when Napoleon was in Elba. At the age of nine, Miss Barrett also traveled in France, in 1815, four months after Waterloo. She undoubtedly had vivid memories of this trip, but not a word—at least an extant word—of it did she write to Haydon. Nor did she discuss her friends and family in much detail. Actually she expatiated more frequently upon Flush, her dog.

They argued politely on two subjects—Napoleon versus Wellington and mesmerism. Although fascinated by Napoleon, Haydon always championed Wellington, but Miss Barrett clung to the romantic hero-worship shown in her poem "Crowned and Buried," inspired by Napoleon's reinterment in Paris in 1840. Haydon scoffed at mesmerism, having attended a séance which was obviously fraudulent and having withstood the efforts of an American to "animal magnetize" him. Miss Barrett, however, was only partially agnostic on the subject at this time. Her belief in spiritualism grew after her marriage despite the utter skepticism of Browning.

After Haydon's death, Miss Barrett's letters were returned to her. Although she disapproved of Harriet Martineau's anathematizing the publication of private letters, claiming that she valued letters as an intrinsic part of biography, she either destroyed or lost a number of them and parts of others, for the collection now at Wellesley College consists only of eighteen complete letters and three fragments. These were sold at Sotheby's in May 1913 after the death of the Brownings' son, Robert Wiedemann Barrett Browning, familiarly known as "Pen." Passing through several hands, they were eventually acquired by Professor George Herbert Palmer, who presented them to Wellesley, in memory of his wife, a former president of that college. The letters were edited by Professor Martha Hale Shackford and published by the Oxford University Press in 1939. Wellesley College has granted permission for their present publication, and the late Sir John Murray, who owned Mrs. Browning's copyright, approved this project, as does his successor in the firm, John Murray, Esq. Unless otherwise noted, the Barrett letters are at Wellesley.

In 1969 Dr. Dallas Pratt presented a valuable collection of manuscripts and memorabilia to the Keats-Shelley Memorial House in Rome, including a letter from Miss Barrett to Haydon (Letter 4) and one from him to her (Letter 9). Part of this letter was reproduced by Sir Sidney Colvin in his *John Keats* (New York, Charles Scribner's Sons, 1925, p. 532), erroneously dated 1834. Both letters were published by Marchesa Iris Origo in her article "Additions to the Keats Collection" *(Times Literary Supplement,* April 23, 1970, pp. 457–458). Permission to publish these letters has been granted by Signora Vera Cacciatore, curator of the Keats-Shelley Memorial House.

Except for the Haydon letter in Rome and three in the Wellesley College Library the others were Lot 17 in the papers of Lieutenant-Colonel Harry Peyton Moulton-Barrett, a nephew of Miss Barrett; they were sold at Sotheby's on June 7, 1937, to Maggs Brothers, and shortly after that date purchased by M. Buxton Forman, Esq., and me. Later I bought Mr. Forman's share and still own the letters. Except for a few quotations in Miss Dorothy Hewlett's *Elizabeth Barrett Browning* (London, Cassell and Company Ltd., 1953), the Haydon letters are heretofore unpublished. The artist's great-grandson, V. Boyd-Carpenter, Esq., approves of this publication.

With minor exceptions, the letters are reproduced *verbatim ac litteratim.* Contracted forms like *shd.*, with a superior *d*, have been expanded, and other superior letters have been aligned. Punctuation has been altered to clarify the meaning of the sentence. Miss Barrett, for example, frequently used three periods in place of a dash; if this punctuation had been used, the reader would believe that an ellipsis was indicated; hence, a dash has been substituted.

I have indicated addresses and postmarks only of letters sent through the mail. Where no such indication appears, I assume that the letters were delivered by hand.

# The Letters

For concise reference in footnotes, the following short titles are used:

*Autobiography. The Autobiography and Memoirs of Benjamin Robert Haydon,* ed. Tom Taylor, a new edition with an introduction by Aldous Huxley; 2 vols. (New York: Harcourt Brace [1926])

*Correspondence. Benjamin Robert Haydon: Correspondence and Table-Talk,* ed. Frederic Wordsworth Haydon, 2 vols. (London: Chatto and Windus, 1876)

*Diary. The Diary of Benjamin Robert Haydon,* ed. Willard Bissell Pope, 5 vols. (Cambridge, Massachusetts: Harvard University Press, 1960–1963)

*Lectures.* Benjamin Robert Haydon, *Lectures on Painting and Design,* 2 vols. (London: Longman, Brown, Green, and Longmans, 1844–1846)

*Letters. The Letters of Elizabeth Barrett Browning,* ed. F. G. Kenyon, 2 vols. (New York: Macmillan, 1897)

Miller. *Elizabeth Barrett to Miss Mitford,* ed. Betty Miller. (London: John Murray, 1954)

Shackford. *Letters from Elizabeth Barrett to B. R. Haydon,* ed. Martha Hale Shackford. (New York: Oxford University Press, 1939)

# 1

## To Haydon
## April 1842

Permit me Sir, to thank you for your kind attention in sending me your interesting & animated treatise on the subject of fresco painting [1] – an attention of which I am abundantly sensible, – though ignorant of practical art & shut out from all especial revelations of *the angel Uriel*, [2] but I can understand the advantage the glorious advantage of a new (old) grand dialect use of the Imaginative faculty – & how, the most imaginative artists being naturally most earnest in aspiration toward such sufficient expression, Mr. Haydon finds himself in heart & voice first in the pursuit. May he find besides success and victory – for the sake of the Houses of Parliament – for the sake of British art, and for the sake of his own fame in its connection.

I count it among my deprivations that I was not able to see him when he did us the kindness of calling here some time ago – but my health unhappily for me, was & is weaker than my will.

It is not possible for me to close this note without saying that I heard from our dear mutual friend Miss Mitford, [3] my very precious friend Miss Mitford a few days since, – & that she speaks with some thing more [of] hope of the infirm state of her father than her anxieties have suffered her to do for a long while past.

I remain Sir

Your obliged & faithful servant

Elizabeth B. Barrett

50 Wimpole Street
April 1842

1. On March 4, 1842, Haydon "lectured at the Royal Institution on Fresco & made a great hit" (*Diary*, V,134). He subsequently published the lecture as *Thoughts on the Relative Value of Fresco and Oil Painting as Applied to the Architectural Decorations of the Houses of Parliament*.

2. An archangel described in *Paradise Lost* (III,690). In 1829, 1844, and 1845 Haydon began oil paintings of "Uriel Revealing himself to Satan," and on August 26, 1841, he wrote to Miss Mitford, describing his first attempt at executing a fresco, with his landlord's permission, on the wall of his painting room. "In four hours," he wrote, "I produced a colossal sketch of 'Uriel disturbed by Satan in disguise of an Angel'" (*Correspondence*, II,137).

3. Mary Russell Mitford (1787–1855), novelist and dramatist, devotedly nursed her extravagant father, George Mitford, M.D., during his long final illness, which ended on December 11, 1842.

# 2

---

## *To Haydon* [1]
## *October 13, 1842*

Dear Sir,

My intention was to return by your messenger when he should come for the picture,[2] some expression of my sense of your very great kindness in trusting it with me,[3] together with this sonnet[4] — but having since heard from my sisters that it may be almost as long as I wish (no! it cant be so long) before you send such a messenger, I cannot defer thanking you beyond today — lest you should fancy me either struck dumb with the pleasure you conferred, or still worse, born an ungrateful person. Pray, dear Sir, believe how different is the reality from the last supposition! I have indeed looked at your picture until I lost my obligation to you in my admiration of your work – but in no other way have I been ungrateful. How could I be so? I have seen the great poet who "reigns over us"[5] twice face to face[6] – & by *you*, I see him the third time. You have brought me Wordsworth & Helvellyn into this dark & solitary room – how should I *not* thank you? Judge for yourself, Mr. Haydon.

But you will judge the *sonnet* too, & will probably not acquit it. It confesses to speaking unworthily & weakly the feeling of its writer – but *she* is none the less,

Your obliged

Elizabeth Barrett B.[7]

A letter from our mutual dear friend Miss Mitford speaks this morning very sadly of her father's state – & I tremble to think what the sacrifice of her filial devotion may cost her in her own health. It is at once admirable & fearful to those who love her.

Mr. Lucas[8] had been talking to her (she says) rapturiusly of your cartoon,[9] *the* cartoon – which I have seen with my ears! – and especially of your Satan. And this rem[inds me tha]t[10] I ought to thank you for [the ticke]ts which admitted my sisters.

October 13th, 1842.
50 Wimpole Street

1. Unpublished letter attached to Haydon's diary. An abridgement of the letter appears at *Correspondence*, I,434.
2. Haydon's "Wordsworth on Helvellyn," now in the National Portrait Gallery.
3. In a letter to Miss Mitford of October 15, 1842, Miss Barrett wrote: "And now I will tell you of a kindness done to me by your friend Mr. Haydon. Henrietta and Arabel both went to see the cartoon ['Adam and Eve'] some days ago . . . and were delighted, full of admiration. He showed them among other pictures, an unfinished portrait of Wordsworth for which he sate this last summer, – and upon the sight of which Arabel exclaimed, – 'Oh, how my sister would like to see this!' 'Then she *shall* see it,' said the kind Mr. Haydon: and accordingly on the very same evening, the picture was sent to me, – and here it is still, because I was desired to keep it until it was sent for. Is it not kind? . . . I mean to send a sonnet back with it as a witness to my feeling" (Miller, p. 135).
4. The holograph of the sonnet is attached to Haydon's diary.

Sonnet

on Haydon's picture of Mr. Wordsworth.    *1842*
Wordsworth upon Helvellyn! Let the cloud
Ebb audibly along the mountain-wind
Then break against the rock, and show behind
The lowland vallies floating up to crowd
The sense with beauty. *He* with forehead bowed
And humble-lidded eyes, as one inclined
Before the sovran thoughts of his own mind
And very meek with inspirations proud, –
Takes here his rightful place as poet-priest
By the high altar, singing prayer & prayer
To the yet higher Heav'ns. A vision free
And noble, Haydon, hath thine art releast.
No portrait this with Academic air!
This is the poet and his poetry.

Elizabeth B. Barrett

Haydon endorsed the holograph, "Very fine – B. R. Haydon." The sonnet was first published in *The Athenaeum* of October 29, 1842, page 932.

5. Cf. "God Save the King," l. 6

6. Miss Barrett met Wordsworth at John Kenyon's house on May 28, 1836, and five days later went with Kenyon, Wordsworth, Miss Mitford, and others to see the Duke of Devonshire's Palladian villa at Chiswick (Miller, pp. viii–x).

7. Elizabeth Barrett Barrett usually signed her name "Elizabeth B. Barrett."

8. John Lucas (1807–1874), portrait painter.

9. "Adam and Eve," painted between July 18 and September 28, 1842, and exhibited in the Cartoon Exhibition, Westminster Hall, June 1843.

10. The conjectural reading is necessitated by a tear in the paper.

# 3

## *To Haydon*
## *October 20, 1842*

Dear Mr. Haydon,

I have sent the sonnet to the Athenaeum & whenever it appears, will do myself the pleasure of forwarding the paper to you. In the meanwhile I hasten to thank you for your very interesting letter.

"Blessings be on them & eternal praise,
    The poets! –" [1]

I like to hear of them—And *you* who are a practical poet, speak of them *with love* as the Italians say. Keats was indeed a fine genius,—too finely tuned for the gross dampness of our atmosphere, the instrument breaking with its own music. As singers sing themselves out of breath, he sang himself out of life—interrupting with death, the perfection & unity of his cadence!—You would rather have walked in Kilburn meadows with Keats,[2] than in palaces, with princes!—And still more—the sympathy & friendship of the consummate, royal poet of our present day must have been well worth to you three cheers of the world, cheering for what it knows not—very well worth its patronage & purple & pence! Whatever may have been the afflictions you speak of,—and trial and struggle come naturally to genius,—I may congratulate you on your destiny. You made me smile with your *theory* about the Athenaeum. The truth is, that the Athenaeum gives all the enthusiasm it has to spare for Art, away from Poetry & Painting to *Music*,—& that moreover, a certain person who writes for it, has a theory too, which he is bound to support under the flashing eyes of all the geniuses of the age,—viz.—that England is worn out & fit for nothing in the world while the world lasts, except paying taxes & travelling thirty miles an hour on the railroad. Yet I think they will admit my sonnet—I do think they will.

If you had not my volume called the *Seraphim*[3] (though the "Seraphim" is almost the worst poem in it) & if you cared to have it, I will ask your acceptance of it. But what am I writing, in the dread presence of *Wordsworth*?

Believe me, sincerely yours<br>Elizabeth B. Barrett

Dr. Mitford remains much in the same state—with occasional rallyings.

Oct. 20. 1842.

1. Wordsworth, "Personal Talk," ll. 51–53. "Blessings be with them—and eternal praise, / Who gave us nobler loves, and nobler cares— / The Poets . . .!"
2. Haydon met John Keats (1795–1821) in 1816. In recording news of his

death, he wrote: "As we were walking along the Kilburn meadows, he repeated this beautiful ode [to a Nightingale], with a tremulous under tone,
that was extremely affecting! I was attached to Keats, & he had great enthusiasm for me" (*Diary*, II,318).

  3. *The Seraphim and Other Poems* (London, Saunders and Otley, 1838).

# 4

---

## *To Haydon* [1]
## *about October 28, 1842*

Dear Mr. Haydon,

  I certainly ought to express my sense of obligation to you
by throwing myself at your feet. Can you guess what pleasure
you have procured me, — you, indirectly? — Guess! *A letter
from Mr. Wordsworth* [2] — Yes indeed! — I had a very kind letter
from him yesterday morning, a letter in his own handwriting
— and if you had not sent him the sonnet (an act which I have
just told him, "simply *confounded* me" at first!) where would
have been my letter? — where my pleasure? — I owe you my
pleasure, Mr. Haydon, & am grateful to you! — I am obliged
to you — obliged to your picture! and the superabundance of
my good humour expends itself even on my sonnet, because
that caught the light of the poet's countenance "as it *fell*."

  Mr. Wordsworth proposes the substitution of

> By a vision free
> And noble, Haydon, is thine art release

for what I wrote: but the criticism came too late to be put to
use. Here is the Athenaeum, — and you will send me in exchange your *theory*. No! — don't send it — because I believe, —
I am afraid, — that the theory is founded upon a truth. The
Athenaeum people spend their enthusiasm upon Thalberg [3]
& his generation, as I have told you — and poets and painters
do not enter into their secret.

  I have to thank you for another copy of the Lecture — and
also for the sight of a very interesting letter to the Sheffield
paper which I seem to be bound to return to you, as you do

not say "keep it." Your ms. letters to myself have scarcely been a means to me of less pleasure — for I delight in all such reminiscences as you tell me of; and your "urn"[4] would be as hallowed in my eyes as any urn which memory leans upon in an allegory — Indeed I do hope to see it some day. But you say "call upon me in the spring" — and I have no business perhaps to think of springs, far less to make engagements for them.

A friend of mine — that is, a friend on paper, — for I correspond with him without having looked ever in his face, Mr. Horne[5] the poet of Cosmo de' Medici — a true poet & most kind friend — knew Keats personally & has often written to me of him. "The divine Keats" he calls him! Very divine — and human — I am sorry that Professor Wilson,[6] himself a man of genius, should have struck an unrighteous blow against Keats, — and I was not aware of the fact until you told me — One dagger was enough, with its base Quarterly[7] plunge — one dagger and exhausted nature! —

[unsigned]

1. Letter presented by Dr. Dallas Pratt of New York to the Keats-Shelley Memorial House in Rome.
2. Dated "Rydal Mount Oct. 26 — 42" (*The Letters of William and Dorothy Wordsworth, the Later Years*, ed. Ernest De Selincourt, Oxford, Oxford University Press, 1939, III,1144–1145).
Writing to Miss Mitford on October 27, 1842, Miss Barrett reported: "Mr. Haydon sent my sonnet to Wordsworth — did I tell you? And to my astonishment, to my great great pleasure this morning, a note very gentle and gracious, from Wordsworth himself was in my hands! I shall throw myself at Mr. Haydon's feet for procuring me such a pleasure! . . . A letter from Wordsworth! Dont tell anybody, but I *kissed* it" (Miller, p. 139).
3. Probably Miss Barrett sent Haydon *The Athenaeum* of October 1, 1842, which contained (p. 853) the following high praise of Sigismund Thalberg (1812-1871), the German pianist and composer: "It must never be forgotten, that for high finish, splendour of tone, and entire and deliberate self-command, we have always rated M. Thalberg as incomparable among the executants." In an enthusiastic review of a concert by Thalberg appearing in *The Athenaeum* of May 21, 1842 (p. 460), the critic wrote: "His tone is still superb; the fullest, richest, most musical sound ever drawn out by keys from wires, — a thing to be admired, and its secret sought by the whole world of pianoforte players."
4. See Letter 41.
5. Richard Henry Horne (1803–1884), best known for his epic *Orion* (1843).
6. John Wilson (1785–1854), author, critic, and professor of moral phi-

losophy at the University of Edinburgh. He collaborated with John Gibson Lockhart in the attacks on "The Cockney School," including Keats, which appeared in *Blackwood's Magazine* in 1817, 1818, and 1819.

7. Miss Barrett referred to John Wilson Croker's savage review of *Endymion* in *The Quarterly Review* of April 1818.

# 5

## *To Haydon*
## *November 5, 1842*

Nov. 5th, 1842

My dear Mr. Haydon,

I am obliged to you, much, for your interesting letter; and you must do me the justice to believe that it did interest me, though I am unlearned in lines & colors, & imprisoned from the sight of them. Yes! I should like to see the pictures you speak of — only I would go first to your fresco, be sure! From what I have heard of the fresco, it must be magnificent! — and then apart from your conception as expressed in it; I never saw any fresco at all, and I have an imagination within me of the probable effect of gigantic creatures floating radiantly along our walls in an atmosphere of their own light! — And then, according to my fancy, the creatures which you conjure for that particular purpose, to live without depth or shadow, ought to be spiritual in a measure at least, removed from the work-day world as far, at least, as your Eve. I fancy, in short, that I shall prefer fresco angels & spirits, to fresco statesmen & heroes. You shake your head, — you will have fresco anything & everything! — and for me, since I speak barely from my fancy & know nothing more about it than my little dog[1] knows, — perhaps silence would become me better than this prating.

Dear Mr. Haydon, I thank you warmly for your praise of my poems. It is very pleasant to me. I love poetry *unto death,* & remember nothing before I loved it — and I do hope sometimes to leave some sign of that love, which shall last, — if my body will but last a little longer. In the poems sent to you, you are probably too well aware of the obscurity with which they have been reproached—obscurity being said to be my haunting fault—but you praise me kindly, instead of "cutting me up." And when you say that my thought about "the pathos in his eyes"[2] will be present with you in your next picture of Christ, you praise me better & more deeply to my satisfaction, than the whole generation of critics could, smiling grimly.

Have you sent the letter?[3] I hope so. I hope also that you considered what I said, said relatively to the best means of proceeding for *you*. As for myself, I would not hesitate to do anything in respect to the business which you pleased—being held in no sort of fear, by that particular critical conclave.

Is it possible? And pray what species of Royal Highness had the knack of making such very wise speeches? or shouldn't I ask such a question? Probably not.

Of the Duke of Sussex,[4] altho' thinking highly, I did not think to the heights of your relation. He is right royal—and that which you have said is the noblest thing I ever heard of him & the most uncommon in the nobleness. Do not scold me dear Mr. Haydon!—I know nothing of German design but I love the Germans.

Ever truly yours,
E. B. Barrett.

I have heard from our dear friend—& Dr. M. remains the same.

---

1. Flush, a red cocker spaniel, which Miss Mitford presented to Miss Barrett in 1841. The dog was stolen four times, to be returned only after ransom of six guineas was paid. He died in Florence in 1854.
2. The quotation is perhaps a reference to Miss Barrett's "The Seraphim," ll. 863–866:
> The pathos hath the day undone:
> The death-look of His eyes
> Hath overcome the sun,
> And made it sicken in its narrow skies. (Shackford, p. 53).
3. Haydon's diary contains drafts of his unpublished letters to Charles Eastlake of October 31 and November 4, 1842, accusing him of pro-German tendencies in designing frescoes (*Diary*, V,216).
4. The Duke of Sussex (1773–1843), sixth son of George III, an acquaintance of Haydon.

# 6

*To Haydon*
*November 6, 1842*

My dear Mr. Haydon:

Your letter interests me very much—the strong *will* of genius is indomptable—& I do not doubt that you are intended to perform the thing you aspire towards. There is nothing nobler to me than resolute genius—nothing nobler in the world! And for the persecution, the oppression, the misconception, these things are constituent conditions of the final triumph, & necessary to the crown. They are natural too. The world is fallen,—and Beauty which is the visible form of Good, cannot enter without struggle near the Evil. Nevertheless you have done much already as Wordsworth is here to testify—and even if you do not do all, you may well repress any feverish impatience with the consideration that earth is not a place for *full* realization even of the Arts. And who knows? There may be grand aerial frescos for archangelic halls, in which thro the great hereafter, you may let out your soul. In the meantime may it have full scope in the English Houses of Parliament.[1]

Dear Mr. Haydon, I shall be very glad to look through the translation which you speak of and to give you my opinion as far as that is worth anything.[2] I am a true lover of Plato[3] & shall be naturally interested in the translation. But for selling—why, without looking at the ms. I can tell you "my thought" as well as if I looked stedfastly—for I do fear that it won't sell. It would be best of course to submit that question to a bookseller; and I anticipate his answer that it won't sell. Plato is too *spiritual* for the Christians of England just now, I am afraid. Will you be angry with me for saying so? Ah, but it is true, I fear, that Jeremy Bentham is fitter for us as a people. Do send me the translation. Shelley was a great poet, but he could not translate Plato, we have more than sufficient evidence.[4]

I congratulate you on having sons to add honor to you—and a daughter,[5] as I understand farther, to realize the visions of your Art.

Alas, no! I do not indeed go out. You must not fancy me a hypochondriac nor even *saddened* with all my solitude. Some three or four years since,[6] I broke a blood-vessel on the chest, & altho' I have rallied at different times & very much for the last year, it is only within these two months that there is evidence of its healing. And even now, I am so weak as to stagger like a drunken man when I attempt to walk without assistance. This however is *strength* comparatively speaking—since at one time, I could not be carried from the bed to the sofa, without dead fainting fits in which it was apprehended that I might pass away. But I believe I am gradually reviving—I think so. And with care & *heat* during the winter, I have hope for next summer. And I tell you all this lest you should think me sulking in my corner away from the sight of your fresco & your Curtius, and your Alexander[7] & the serpent to come!

I have had a letter from our dear Miss Mitford to-day,—& her father lingers still. It is a strange prolongation of life in death—and her spirits, so elastic ordinarily, seem to fail & falter. My dear admirable friend! May God sustain her to the last, & into the solitude beyond it!—

I am glad I did not talk nonsense (quite) about the fresco. I am glad you like the Germans.[8] I am gladdest of all that you deny the alleged obscurity of my poems.

I shall be glad too if you will let me remain, with much estimation,

Faithfully yours,
Elizabeth Barrett B—

50 Wimpole Street
(Nov. 6th 1842

My sisters desire their remembrances to you.

1. The Houses of Parliament were destroyed by fire on October 16, 1834. Haydon entered the competition to choose cartoons for frescoes in the new buildings but learned on June 27, 1843, that his drawings were unsuccessful (*Diary*, V,293).

2. Haydon's stepson, Orlando Hyman (1814–1878), a fellow of Wadham College, Oxford, translated Plato's *Gorgias*. Two sentences are found in the *Diary* (V,214) confirming Miss Barrett's opinion, expressed in a letter of January 5, 1843, to Hugh Boyd. She wrote that "it is an excellent translation . . . , but it is not *elegant*. He [Haydon] means to try the public upon it, but, as I have intimated to him, the Christians of the present day are not civilized enough for Plato" (*Letters*, I,119). Writing to Miss Mitford on November 18, 1842, Miss Barrett expressed a similar opinion (Miller, p. 143).

3. Miss Barrett revealed her love for Plato in a letter of March 5, 1842, to Hugh Boyd, writing, "when three years ago, and a few months previous to my leaving home, I became possessed of a complete edition of his [Plato's] works, edited by Bekker, why then I began with the first volume and went through the whole of his writings, with those I knew and those I did not know, one after another: and have at this time read, not only all that is properly attributed to Plato, but even those dialogues and epistles which pass falsely under his name—everything except two books I think, or three, of the treatise 'De Legibus,' which I shall finish in a week or two" (Shackford, p. 54).

4. Shelley's translations of the *Symposium* and *Ion* were published by Mary Shelley in 1841.

5. Haydon had eight children, five of whom died in infancy before 1836. The survivors were Frank Scott Haydon (1822–1887), who at this time held a scholarship at Jesus College, Cambridge; Frederic Wordsworth Haydon (1827–1886), a midshipman in the navy; and Mary Mordwinoff Haydon (1824–1864).

6. Actually in 1838.

7. The fresco was "The Black Prince Entering London in Triumph," and the other pictures were "Curtius Leaping into the Gulf" and "Alexander's Combat with the Lion."

8. Haydon disliked German paintings and deplored the influence he felt German artists exerted in England. Professor Shackford (p. 54) believed he had referred to his admiration for Goethe and Karl Friedrich von Rumohr, an art collector and critic with whom Haydon corresponded in 1842 and 1843.

# 7

---

## To Haydon
## November 29, 1842

My dear Mr. Haydon,

I wish I could hear your Lectures [1] — but I can only read your letters & thank you for them heartily — & for the *hope of*

*Curtius!* How kind to me you are!—Shall you print the Lectures[2]—so that I may read them?

Yes! The permission of *Evil* is a mystery—and all that argument & egotism of men have done to make it clear, have simply left it more mysterious. I never however, I thank God for it, doubted of the power of God—I never do. God *could* (be sure) breathe aside this evil, as the least cloud from a summer sky. His power could annihilate it. His wisdom leaves it. But it is *we* who cannot comprehend His wisdom.

Of the permission of evil, I have sometimes thought painfully, as others have: and my idea, my fancy is, that it was *necessary* in order to the communication to a finite nature of the consciousness of good. An infinite Being like the Creator sees the essential & the abstract object; but we who are finite understand nothing except by comparison & contrast. Referring to our daily experience we may observe that we discern nothing in the external world except by the help of *two colours*.[3] If there were no color but one shade of green,—whatever might be the variety of form, we should see only one great green flat—no lines, no angles, no difference between hill & valley, or Heaven & earth. And this being so in the material, it is also so in the spiritual. Adam in his first day's joy, was good & happy, undiscerningly, unconsciously; his goodness was his life, & not his choice & preference & glory. He knew nothing of his good. He was blind & deaf to it. The *knowledge* of it came with the knowledge of evil—& was the fruit of the same tree. After all *what is evil?* Do we know more of *that*, then of its origin?

What is evil? *Sin*—and a blank! Presently, & in another state of being, what we have called evil here, may shine out to us as good & blessing,—& what we have delighted in as good, may fall from the appellation. Then at least we shall comprehend the unity & harmony of all these apparent discords!—and then, standing farther from the picture which now we touch with our eyelashes, we shall lose sight of these roughnesses & unevennesses, & acknowledge the beauty of the work, & the power & consistent skill of the artist. May it be so to you dear Mr. Haydon, fully & joyfully! – In the meantime, there is noble work for you to do.

Poor Dr. Mitford remains in much the same state.

Ever sincerely yours

Elizabeth B. Barrett

Nov. 29 1842

1. Haydon wrote in his diary for November 24, 1842, "Lectured tonight – second time this year, at London Institution – to a brilliant Audience."
2. Haydon published the first volume of his *Lectures on Painting and Design* in 1844 and the second in 1846.
3. Miss Barrett expressed a similar idea in her letter to R. H. Horne of December 13, 1843 (Shackford, p. 55).

# 8

*To Haydon*[1]
*December 8, 1842*

My dear Mr. Haydon,

I wont betray your confidence – either for past present or future – and I agree with you that Milton's Hell was a sight worth seeing.

And so is your Arab – & the suggestion of Curtius. What an eye in the Arab! – not so much startled as *ready to startle*. Is the nostril quite sensitive in proportion? I wonder if it is. I am not accomplished for a critic, & if I were you might well frown away any critical impertinence – but – it does strike me that the nostril is at once meeker & calmer than the eye is – forgive me!

I have looked at it till I should not be astonished if it neighed. Yet the nostril would swell even then – yes, *certainly then!* – "but not now" you say. Well!

How kind of you my dear Mr. Haydon to trust these fine things with me. Who shall say that I am alone now? Why here is Wordsworth – & Quintus Curtius – and when I grow weary of that high company, an Arab charger to ride away on.

Curtius looks noble & serene amidst the yawning death — & the horse is just losing, I see, his balance in the leap — the head sinking between the fore-legs, the hind quarters still with the glory of the spring in them — and the tail streaming grandly with a look of life & triumph. The picture must be magnificent. And your kindness — your kindness! — how am I to thank you for *that*?

I had a very few words from our dear friend this morning. She says — "His sad scene is drawing to a close. All day I have been hovering over my dear dear father. He is composed & tranquil, but has not spoken. Certainly he does not suffer & Mr. May[2] says that he has seldom seen a death-bed so blessedly peaceful. I am myself more supported than I had dared to hope."

May God comfort her — & let us pray that He may.

I never saw Dr. Mitford — but I feel for her sake as if I knew & regarded him.

Ever your obliged<br>Elizabeth B. Barrett

Dec. 8, 1842.

1. Unpublished letter attached to Haydon's diary.
2. George May was the Mitford's family physician.

# 9

### To Miss Barrett [1]
### before December 29, 1842 [2]

Keats' expression too subtle for the Brush! — there's a *pretty confession* — there is nothing too subtle for the brush, — one night I made a sketch of him on condition he would make one of me[3] — I'll send you a repetition (not *the one under*) but a regular copy [*a profile sketch of Keats, with two canceled sketches*].

Something like—you shall have a right one.

His expression was exquisite poor dear Keats—I put him in my great Picture of Jerusalem[4] now at Philadelphia.

Never shall I forget one day at Hampstead—Leigh Hunt invited a large party to breakfast, I was lodging at Hampstead for bad health & was invited, as I knew the poetical irregularity of Hunt's domesticities I told Keats I should breakfast *before* I went & be over about 11—saying I'll bet 5 to 1 by that time you will not have seen the breakfast Cloth.

At 11 I walked over & found Keats and a party patrolling before the House on the grass, in doleful sarcasm, as they had been there two hours without a morsel—I laughed ready to drop & said What's the matter, for this is worse than usual— Oh said Keats his Wife's Sister, who is in love with Hunt, tried to drown herself this morning in one of the ponds, and it was so shallow, she only tumbled in the black mud, & has just gone in covered, being pulled out by *two laborers!*

After walking, I took my leave, & believe about one— they got their breakfast—Keats called on me after—& we revelled—

He bitterly lamented his intimacy with that incarnate Vanity—as I have done all my life—for he injured me, Keats, & did Byron great harm—There never was born such a mixture & incarnation of Conceit, impudence, talent, ignorance, malice, geniality, amiability, affectation & scepticism with sufficient glimpses of belief to make him afraid of damnation as Leigh Hunt. He disbelieved Christianity, & had too much of the Cockney not to be afraid of the Devil.

B. R. Haydon

I meant you to keep the Manuscript—shall I inscribe it & send it back?[5]

I shall send for 2 of the Sketches, in a day or two about *one* in the day.

*Address:* Miss B. Barrett / 50 Wimpole St
*Postmark:* illegible.

1. Letter presented by Dr. Dallas Pratt to the Keats-Shelley Memorial House in Rome. Part of it is reproduced as plate XIII, facing page 532, in Sidney Colvin's *John Keats* (New York, Charles Scribner's Sons, 1925), with the caption, "Page from a letter of Benjamin Robert Haydon to Elizabeth Barrett, 1834."

2. Colvin erroneously dated the letter 1834, some eight years before the Haydon-Barrett Correspondence began. It should be dated before December 29, 1842, when Miss Barrett's letter to Horne "with 'a pen-and-ink profile of Keats' at the head, began: 'Tell me, Mr. Horne — is it like? to Keats, I mean. My hands have ague this morning. Otherwise it would be a copy of a sketch of Keats; and I want to know if you have any recognition.' This probably was copied by Miss Barrett from the drawing, in Haydon's letter to her, reproduced [by Colvin]" (Shackford, p. 52).

3. Haydon's profile of Keats, dated "Nov. 1816," and the "vile caricature of B. R. Haydon by John Keats," originally on facing pages in Haydon's diary, are now in the National Portrait Gallery.

4. Haydon included portraits of Keats, Wordsworth, and Hazlitt among the crowd in "Christ's Entry into Jerusalem," painted between 1814 and 1820. When he wrote this letter the picture was being exhibited at the Academy of Fine Arts in Philadelphia; it is now in Saint Gregory's Seminary, Cincinnati.

5. Haydon gave Miss Barrett sixteen lines (ll. 227–242) of Keats's manuscript of "I Stood Tiptoe," writing at the foot of the paper, "A Fragment of Dear Keats poetry & writing, given to me by him & by me to Miss Barrett December 30, 1842. B. R. Haydon." It is curious that Miss Barrett did not mention the gift in her reply to this letter.

# 10

## To Haydon
## January 1, 1843

Jany. 1. 1843.

My dear Mr. Haydon

If I am a stone, I am a stone, you probably think; & there's an end of me in cases of wooden pavement. Not to write for so long! — Not to be wakened up by the sight of your pictures! But there, you err! For I *am* wakened up by your pictures! [1]

Thank you much, much, for your kindness in permitting me to look at them. They are fine in different ways. Curtius fulfils my idea from your first sketch — and it strikes me that you have happily seized the balance of the moment when the horse begins to sink, — losing his muscular command, &

power of animal life, — while the man-will reins right royally unto death. The other picture contains a grand thought which "the world will not let die." I ought not to upbraid you after all with Napoleon. You have done him noble homage. You have been one of the kings in his antechambers — have you not? Who can deny it?

Talking of kings & their fashions; when you proposed to me to "exchange portraits royally," it was necessary first of all that there should be a portrait of each of us in existence.

Two years ago when I was in Devonshire, & my chances appeared small of ever returning,[2] I admitted a Mrs. Carter[3] a miniature painter to my bedroom, & she made a portrait of me for "Papa" —[4] which, because it isn't like, there can be no use in sending for your examination. For *I* say it is flattering & *he* says it is libelling, & both of us are right in a way; the features being better & more regular than mine, & the expression more indicative perhaps of — "My Damon! I am sick" than I have pastoral sentiment for! — That it isn't like altogether, we agree — & thus I can't send it for you to see; and besides, I am not a King — & besides, I mean to try to be remembered by my soul rather than by my body; which last (in confidence) is not worth much of your enquiry. I would not be engraved for some publishers who asked me the other day, — I am sick of bodies for my part. Except for my body, should I not have seen your Alexander before now? Certainly I owe it a grudge — & have half a mind to draw it for you and avenge myself. But no! Yet to give scanty data to your fancy; thus, — I am "little & black" like Sappho,[5] en attendant the immortality — five feet one high; as to the latitude, straight to correspond — eyes of various colours as the sun shines, — called blue & black, without being accidentally black & blue — affidavit-ed for grey — sworn at for hazel — & set down by myself (according to my "private view" in the glass) as dark-green-brown — grounded with brown, & green otherwise; what is called "invisible green" in invisible garden-fences. I should be particular to you who are a colourist. Not much nose of any kind; certes no superfluity of nose; but to make up for it, a mouth suitable to a larger personality – oh, and a very very little voice, to which Cordelia's was a happy medium.[6] Dark hair and complexion. Small face & sundries.

Whereupon, terrified by the image of a green eyed monster, you start back, & I break off suddenly. Sic periit gloria foeminarum!

Faithfully yours
Elizabeth B Barrett

I have been and am very busy – & have not been well with cold etc.

Bear in mind how I thank you for the pictures – ! And your card – they brought it up to me – ! –

1. Haydon had already lent Miss Barrett sketches of "Curtius Leaping into the Gulf." At this time he seems to have sent her his third oil painting of the subject, completed on December 15, 1842, and one of his oils of "Napoleon Musing at St. Helena." Of twenty-three paintings of this subject, he had already completed six.

2. Believing that residence in Devonshire would improve her health, Miss Barrett went to Torquay in 1838 and remained there for three years. In July 1840 her favorite brother, Edward Barrett, was drowned near Torquay. The shock overwhelmed her.

3. Matilda Carter, wife of the portrait painter J. H. Carter, was a miniaturist who frequently exhibited at the Royal Academy between 1839 and 1869. She died in 1891.

4. On October 5, 1843, Miss Barrett wrote to Richard H. Horne: "And yet, although she [Mrs. Carter] was so obliging as to paint a very pretty little girl with unexceptionable regularity of features, he was ungrateful enough to throw it down with a pshaw! and deny the likeness altogether. There is no portrait of me at all which is considered like – except one painted in my infancy, where I appear in the character of a fugitive angel, which papa swears by all his gods is very like me to this day, and perhaps may be like – about the wings" (Shackford, pp. 55–56).

5. The description of Sappho is traditionally derived from Ovid's *Epistle of Sappho to Phao*. The passage occurs in the *Heroides*, XV,33–36 (Shackford, p. 56).

6. *King Lear*, V,iii,271–273. "Cordelia, Cordelia! stay a little. Ha! / ... Her voice was ever soft, / Gentle, and low; an excellent thing in woman."

# 11

<hr>

### To Miss Barrett
### early January 1843 [1]

My dear Miss Barrett

I entrust you with what no human eye but my own has seen — tell me *frankly* your opinion of it, and if it be readable you shall see the rest. I want the Horse's head & the Fiend's head (the White Horse) — pray consider the manuscript sacredly confidential — I fear the journal *can't* be sent.

Yours<br>B. R. H.

1. Miss Barrett replied to this on January 8, 1843 (Letter 12).

# 12

<hr>

### To Haydon
### January 8, 1843

Your autobiography my dear Mr. Haydon is delightful! [1] I have been deeply interested in it in all ways — & I do trust that the day is not distant when with the suppression of an unmeasured word or two, you will take the public into your confidence & throw wide the pleasure. It appears to me that you *should do it* — that you owe this MS. to the world as you owe to it the productions of your Art — the spectacle of the life-agony, (if I may use such an expression) of a gifted mind being a no less noble & exalting sight to look on, than any shewn by canvas or fresco. No irreverence to the brush in this! — But be sure of it! —

The scene between the mother & son — where genius carries it over love – was very affecting to me![2] – and the descriptions of Northcote, Opie, & Fuseli are highly graphic & life like.[3]

Dear Mr Haydon – I value more the *confidence*, the more I see to value in its bestower. Pray give me some more MS. I could read a thousand miles of it.

Ever sincerely yours,<br>Elizabeth B Barrett

Jany. 8, 1843.

If you send me any more MS. fold it in a larger sheet – will you? – as I have done – otherwise there is a risk in opening the seals of tearing the written paper – *as I have done* – in one place I fear! – Nobody has seen a passage of it. Nobody inhabits this room with me, to look over my shoulder – always excepting my little spaniel Flush & *he can't read* – the only thing impossible to him!

1. Haydon began his *Autobiography* on July 7, 1839; at the time of his death in 1846, however, he had progressed only as far as 1820.

2. "I collected my books and colours – packed my things – an on the 13th of May, 1804, took my place in the mail for the next day. The evening was passed in silent musing. Affection for home was smothered, not extinguished in me: I thought only of *London* – Sir Joshua – Drawing – Dissection – and High Art.

"The next day I ate little, spoke less, and kissed my mother many times. When all my things were corded and packed ready for the mail, I hung about my mother with a fluttering at my heart, in which duty, affection and ambition were struggling for the mastery.

"As evening approached I missed my mother. At last the guard's horn announced the coming mail; I rushed upstairs, called her dear name, and was answered only by violent sobbings from my own bedroom. She could not speak – she could not see me. 'God bless you, my dear child,' I could just make out in her sobbings. The guard became impatient; I returned slowly downstairs with my heart too full to speak, shook my father by the hand, got in, the trunks were soon on the top, the whip cracked, the horses pranced and started off – my career for life had begun!" (*Autobiography*, I,16).

3. James Northcote (1746–1831), R.A., worked as an assistant to Sir Joshua Reynolds, about whom he published a memoir. He painted nine pictures for the Boydel Shakespeare Gallery but is known primarily as a portrait painter. John Opie (1761–1807), R.A., was a successful portrait and historical painter. Henry Fuseli (1741–1825), R.A., was born in Zurich but resided in England after 1763. A student of Greek sculpture and of Michelangelo, he was professor of painting at the Royal Academy from 1799 until his death.

Haydon thus described his meeting with these artists: "[Prince Hoare] gave me letters to Northcote and to Opie; Northcote being a Plymouth man, I felt a strong desire to see him first.

"I went . . . I was shown first into a dirty gallery, then upstairs into a dirtier painting-room, and there, under a high window with the light shining full on his bald grey head, stood a diminutive wizened figure in an old blue-striped dressing-gown, his spectacles pushed up on his forehead. Looking keenly at me with his little shining eyes, he opened the letter, read it, and with the broadest Devon dialect said: 'Zo, you mayne tu bee a peinter doo-ee? what zort of peinter?' 'Historical painter, sir,' 'Heestoricaul peinter! why yee'll starve with a bundle of straw under yeer head!' . . .

"I was not disconcerted, . . . and off I walked to Opie, who lived in Berners Street. I was shown into a clean gallery of masculine and broadly painted pictures. After a minute down came a coarse-looking intellectual man. He read my letter, eyed me quietly, and said: 'You are studying anatomy — master it — were I your age, I would do the same.' My heart bounded at this; I said: 'I have just come from Mr. Northcote, and he says I am wrong, sir.' 'Never mind what *he* says,' said Opie; 'he doesn't know it himself, and would be very glad to keep you as ignorant.' I could have hugged Opie . . .

"Prince Hoare told me that he had seen Fuseli, who wished me to call on him with my drawings . . .

"I followed [the maid] into a gallery or showroom, enough to frighten anybody at twilight. Galvanised devils — malicious witches brewing their incantations — Satan bridging Chaos, and springing upward like a pyramid of fire — Lady Macbeth — Paolo and Francesca — Falstaff and Mrs. Quickly — humour, pathos, terror, blood, and murder, met one at every look! I expected the floor to give way — I fancied Fuseli himself to be a giant. I heard his footsteps and saw a little bony hand slide round the edge of the door, followed by a little white-headed lion-faced man in an old flannel dressing-gown tied round his waist with a piece of rope and upon his head the bottom of Mrs. Fuseli's work-basket" (*Autobiography*, I,19–22).


# 13

## To Miss Barrett
## January 9, 1843

London Jan 9 1843

My dear Invisible Friend, are you convinced I am mad? I fear the memoirs will confirm it — It was a confidential confiding, & therefore ought to be considered only what it is — the gradual progress of thought, perception & sensation — only suppose we are never to see each other! — as long as we

live, always to correspond & never to speak, never to descend
to the Vulgarity of speaking; I am delighted at the Idea, but
don't keep me on the rack about the manuscript—if there be
anything a delicate mind ought not to be subjected to—make
allowance—

Ever yours<br>
BRH

*Address:* Miss B. Barrett / 50 Wimpole St
*Postmark:* JA 10 1843

## 14

---

*To Miss Barrett*
*January 14, 1843*

London Jan 14 1843

Dear Miss Barrett,

Am I not a beauty for a compliment?—I had a glimpse it
was a *beauty* of a compliment when I was writing but I knew
you would see what I meant, which was nothing but a bit of
imagination; there is something so original in a couple of
Geniuses corresponding, becoming acquainted, knowing each
other thoroughly & yet never seeing each other, that I revelled
in the Idea beyond expression—

You must take my manuscript as I wrote it—hurriedly—
& without revision—if there be any thing you ought not to
see—I had not time to supervise—Yours ever &c.

B. R. Haydon

*Address:* Miss Barrett / 50 Wimpole St
*Postmark:* JA 16 1843

# 15

## To Miss Barrett
## January 24, 1843

Tuesday Night Jan 24. 1843

Dear Miss Barrett,

Your flattering interest in my memoirs, is very delightful—
I have written no more consecutively—but you encourage me
—should the year & dates be given—would it make it clearer?
—you are coming to the beginning of the anxieties of my
Life—

Sir George *refused* Macbeth after 3 years labor—relying on
his honor I *borrowed* to complete it. By his refusal, I lost the
great prize to which I was entitled 300 gs—his price 500 gs—
and at 26 years of age I was disappointed of 800 gs, which
would have established my fortune![1]—from that hour to
this my Life has been a long struggle.

Dentatus the Academy placed in the great Room where it
looked powerfully—they removed it to the dark—ruined me
with my Patrons. The next year I sent it to the Gallery where
it won the great prize—and again I was the fashion!![2] Sir
George when Solomon came out gave me another order of
*200 gs*—I told him to take Macbeth for 200 gs. which *he did,*
hung it up where he said he had not room for it—he lent it
to me for Exhibition with my other Works—It was the only
Picture seized in my ruin—& he spent 360—in a Chancery
suit *to keep it!*—saying no compensation in money would
compensate your orator, for *such a work of art!*—A Work
he refused! To the day of his Death[3] it haunted him—& the
last letter he ever wrote to Lord Farnborough, one whole side
was devoted to giving a high opinion of me—the day after
he died!

Poor dear Sir George—with no Man have I spent more delightful days—he was my bane & my blessing—had he kept
his word I should never have been embarrassed! no Man had
brighter prospects—no Man had been less offensive but this

abominable treatment exasperated my nature – and I became a fierce ungovernable leader of forlorn hopes!

I will continue my life – Dissenter or Democrat it is no matter to me – but Monarchy will be the ruling Government of the Earth in the long run – and if you do not believe in the Divinity of Christ – I wish you did.

God bless you<br>B. R. Haydon

*Address:* Miss B. Barrett / 50 Wimpole Street
*Postmark:* JA 25 1843

1. Haydon inaccurately recalled his controversy with Sir George Beaumont concerning his first painting of "Macbeth," exhibited at the British Institution in 1812 in competition for prizes of three hundred, two hundred, and one hundred guineas. The first two prizes were withdrawn to permit the Royal Academy to purchase for five hundred guineas Henry James Richter's "Christ Healing the Blind," and the third prize was awarded to George Francis Joseph's "Procession to Mount Calvary" (*Autobiography*, I,135–136).

Although Haydon insisted that he had commissioned a full-sized picture, Sir George maintained that he had wanted a smaller one. Many letters on the subject were exchanged before May 20, 1816, at which time Sir George gave Haydon two hundred guineas for the picture (*Autobiography*, I,244). In 1823, when Sir George had lent it to Haydon to be exhibited with other pictures, it was seized by sheriff's officers while Haydon was in debtors' prison.

2. "The Assassination of Dentatus" was exhibited at the Royal Academy in 1809. Originally hung in the Great Room, it was removed to an anteroom (*Autobiography*, I,87). On May 17, 1810, the picture was awarded a premium of one hundred guineas from the British Institution.

3. February 7, 1827.

# *16*

---

## *To Miss Barrett*
## *January 25, 1843*

London Jan 25 1843

My dearest Friend

Your letter is an honor to your heart & genius, had I recollected your Poetry *that moment*, I could not have said it – Let it pass for ever –

Tell me *all* you object to in your feelings of my life – because your criticism will be valuable & Useful –

Good Heaven – dear Mary Mitford I'll do all I can in every way, I have no doubt, it will succeed & extricate her[1] – I thought from what Sergeant Talfourd said, she was independent, when all was paid – I feel for her, poor dear soul, as she felt for me – I will write her directly –

My subject is Edward the Black Prince entering London with John Prisoner [*a sketch of this subject*]. I send you a sketch which will explain to you – the composition.

I am My dear Friend
B. R. Haydon

*Address:* Miss B. Barrett / 50 Wimpole Street
*Postmark:* JA 26 1843

1. Dr. George Mitford died on December 11, 1842, nearly a thousand pounds in debt. A public subscription oversubscribed this amount, and all creditors were paid (W. J. Roberts, *Mary Russell Mitford*, London, Andrew Melrose, 1913, pp. 361–363).

# 17

*To Miss Barrett*
*January 27, 1843*

London Jan 27th 1843

My dear Miss Barrett
Your advice about Liz[1] shall be attended to – or any other you will give – shall I divide into dates? – & years? –

I shall exchange your sketches shortly – to amuse you –
Yours ever
B. R. Haydon

I have been working with intense delight all day – & successfully – Heaven knows my fate! The World has a singular relish to thwart a Man when what he has sought all his life, is getting into his grasp—This summer will settle it—I think you will like the Cartoons in the Spring or the Summer, when ever it be you make your debut again.

I wrote Mary Mitford yesterday.

Dear Madam, what an affliction it must have been to have so overwhelmed your soul—you did not see a last look[2]—there is nothing like it—there are two things, you are convinced are supernatural on Earth, a *last look*—& the throtled scream that launches another creature into this breathing world[3]—

There is nothing like *that* in Heaven or Hell.

Good night—or I shall get poetical—

*Address:* Miss B. Barrett / 50 Wimpole St.
*Postmark:* JA 28 1843

1. If Miss Barrett advised excision of references to "Liz," Haydon disregarded her and included in his *Autobiography* (I,54–56) vivid accounts of evenings with his fellow students and "an attractive girl on the second floor of a house full of young men . . . She attached herself to the party, made tea for them, marketed for them, carved for them, went to the play with them, read Shakespeare with them . . . Liz was as interesting a girl as you would wish to see, and very likely to make a strong impression on anyone that knew her; however, I kept clear, and she ultimately married the Frenchman [Du Fresne]."
2. Edward Barrett visited his sister in Torquay in the summer of 1840. On July 11 he went sailing with two friends; the sea was calm, but an accident occurred and he drowned. Although she was blameless, a great feeling of guilt intensified her grief.
3. Haydon refers to the birth of his first child, Frank Scott Haydon, on December 12, 1822. "Never to my dying day shall I forget the dull, throtled scream of agony, that preceded the birth, and then the infant cry that announced its completion" (*Diary*, II,393).

# 18

---

## To Miss Barrett
## January 31, 1843

London Jan 31, 1843
at Night

My dearest Friend,

Chaucer shall be as surely in my Cartoon[1] as the black Prince and I have a great mind to beat my own head for not thinking of him before you.

I introduce the *Fool* also *quizzing* the whole human triumph, and that's as good as your Chaucer—I shall send for the Bust the moment I want it.

Between us both we will make a fine thing—but don't you be frightened at others—

Yours ever & ever
B. R. Haydon

*Address:* Miss B. Barrett / 50 Wimpole Street
*Postmark:* FE 1 1843

1. "The Black Prince Entering London in Triumph," on which Haydon was engaged from May 10, 1842, to March 15, 1843. The Black Prince took the French king, Jean II, prisoner at the Battle of Poitiers (1356) and brought him to London the following year. Chaucer is included among the spectators.

# 19

---

## To Haydon
## February 7, 1843

I congratulate you my dear friend upon the Curtius. The Morning Chronicle gives me good news of it as the finest work of art in the exhibition[1]—and my cousin Mr. Kenyon,[2] with whom I talked of it yesterday, said that it was a "grand conception" — praised the "serene look (not exaggerated in serenity — )" of the hero; & the wild, plunging turbulence of the horse — & observed that you almost tremble while you look at it lest you should be overwhelmed bodily by man & horse. You may be certain how much pleasure I feel in your success

> — moi qui ne suis rien
> Pas même Academicien! —

& how, although I cannot see it, I imagine the grandeur of the contrast & antithesis between that calm human will & that violent animal agony! —

Thank you for acceding to my thought about Chaucer. Your Fool is excellent — *There*, too, will be antithesis! — And if your mind is to be generous & admit Gower, — *why not?* — & going upon a pilgrimage to St. Saviour's Church Southwark you will find him in monumental effigies, ready to be painted from.[3]

Most truly yours — between this & my monument. —

Elizabeth B. Barrett

Feb. 7th. 1843

1. Haydon showed "Curtius Leaping into the Gulf" at the British Institution's exhibition of 1843. It is now in the Royal Albert Memorial Museum, Exeter.
2. John Kenyon (1784–1856), poet and philanthropist.
3. Gower is buried in an elaborate grave surmounted by a full-sized effigy in the Church of St. Saviour.

# 20

*To Miss Barrett*
*February 9, 1843*

London Feb 9 1843

Dearest Friend,

I am delighted you & your Cousin are pleased—I believe it to be one of my most Successful Conceptions, & executions—Oh for 20 years Health, Sight & Brain my dear Miss Barrett!—

I have had some letters from Sir Samuel Meyrick,[1] he says Chaucer was 17—& Gower 27—as Chaucer said when under examination as a Witness he was 40 years old 1386—this is very interesting—Gower shall go in but I fear I must put them both looking at the Sight on a balcony as they would not be in a Crowd—Can you lend me Chaucer's works?—what is there of Gower to read—I am ignorant of my own Country in these points having dwelt more on Greek & Roman.

There is not enough of the Naked for me—It is all Costume & armour, & fleurs de lis & heraldic Lions—the faces & expressions & incidents are fine, but the Climate destroys the figure by Cloaks & Coifs, & Wimples, & hoods—the naked Majesty of Nature is ruined.

I know Chaucer & think him an exquisite Genius—full of Nature fresh—pure, vigorous & simple.

Sir Samuel Meyrick seems brimming full of knowledge in such matters, and very kind—

Where can I get a likeness of Gower in what [?] Monumental Effigies?

If your Cousin or any of your Friends would like to see my Cartoons any Sunday from 2 till 4—I need not say how happy I shall be—

I have done the Prince's *Pony*. I met a beauty in St. James St. black & full of blood, & got the address—I have half done—the Trumpeter's horse in the Blues is to be the King John's—that I go for to-morrow—I feel wings in my right hand!—I wish I was loose in St. Paul's Dome—Oh you dear Invisible Friend, I should soon make you come out! Shall I send you down a Portfolio of studies, sketches & all sorts of things?— Shall I send you my early book of anatomical studies, which Eastlake the Landseers & Lance[2] & all my Pupils [used] and which really has been the basis of a reform?—All this will amuse you & you may keep each 3 days—

Tell me, I never see your Sisters, any Sunday I shall be most happy, or any of your family—or Friends—

Ever Thine faithfully
B. R. Haydon

*Address:* Miss B. Barrett / 50 Wimpole St.
*Postmark:* FE 10 1843

1. Sir Samuel Rush Meyrick (1783–1848), antiquary. Five letters from him to Haydon are included in *Correspondence*, I,435–439.
2. Charles Eastlake (1793–1865); Charles (1799–1879), Thomas (1795–1880), and Edwin (1802–1873) Landseer; and George Lance (1802–1864) were among Haydon's pupils.

# 21

---

## *To Haydon*
## *February 11, 1843*

My dear Friend,

Old Winstanley who writes of the poets, says of Gower—"He was buried at St. Mary Overies at Southwark, on the north side of the said church in the chapel of St. John . . . He lieth under a tomb of stone, with his image also of stone over him, the haire of his heade auburn, long to his shoulders, but curling up, and a smalle forked bearde; [on his head a Chaplet] like a coronet of four roses; an habit of purple damasked down to his feet, a collar of esses of gold about his neck, which being proper to places of judicature, makes some think he was a judge in his old age." [1] His English poem, the only work by which he is known, is the "*Confessio amantis*" consisting of various tales told with simplicity & some grace & tenderness. If it were not that the sound of Chaucer's music puts out his, we should run more eagerly to praise him. Chaucer calls him "the morall Gower" [2] in one place, & says "fye" to his "cursed stories" [3] in another – but on the ground of delicacy the poets may stand side by side as in your balcony. [4] I wish I could send you the "Confessio amantis" – I have read it but do not possess it – & have been waiting for some time until a black letter copy shall fall within reach of my hands.

Sir Samuel Meyrick is as high an authority upon all matters of antiquity, that I am half afraid of expressing to you my very large doubt upon his view of Chaucer's age. [5] Leland [6] has been convicted of making the poet too young – and the general inference of the critics goes with the testimony of the monument erected to him by Brigham [7] in 1555 according to the previous testimony of his disciple the poet Occleve [8] – & this testimony states the period of his death as October 1400. Now that he died an *old man,* is evident from his writings, and if he was 40 in 1386 he could have been only 54 in 1400, which is by no means old. Moreover Gower at the close of his "*Confessio amantis*" represents Venus as desiring Chaucer

> "To putte an ende of alle his work
> As one who is my oldë clerk." [9]

*After* which, Chaucer, so far from putting an end to his work, wrote the "Canterbury Tales" his greatest production, in order to prove what "the oldë clerke" could do.

I do not wish to involve you in a controversy, my dear Mr. Haydon – and a few years, more or less, will make no great difference to your picture. My own creed is that Chaucer was born somewhere about 1328, – which would bring him nearly to thirty when your French king was brought into London on the white horse "with very rich furniture" [10] – & that Gower was not much – not by many years – his senior. John of Gaunt & Chaucer were fast friends.

I send you my black letter Chaucer,[11] & also Mr. Horne's edition of a modernized selection in which Mr. Wordsworth, Leigh Hunt, & others less worthy, were fellow-workers.[12] If you look to the "Prologue" as it is called of "Sir Thopas," page 109, you will find Chaucer's description of his own "elvish countenance,"[13] There is a picture of him at Oxford — but that is drawn I believe from a portrait in certain mss belonging to the Marquis of Stafford.[14] Do you know him? Ah! — if you had access to *those*?

There is a great deal more to say — & yet, perhaps, nothing which is likely to be of use to you. Is Sir Samuel Meyrick's tradition of a signature a proof that the poet did not *choose to be old*? Certainly, I always did fancy that he quarrelled with Gower for calling him an "old clerk"! — I always fancied so — & said so in the Athenaeum once![15] — it would be curious if we could prove *that*. But perhaps this is simply *a ladylike notion* of mine — & high treason against my Master.

Thank you for your kindness about the frescos — for *all* your kindness — & of course I say "yes" to the *portfolios*, & will tell Mr. Kenyon.

Ever yours<br>EBB

Saturday. Feb. 1843

Is "St. Mary Overies at Southwark" the same as St. Saviour's at Southwark?[16] Perhaps so. You will deserve well of your country if you [can] force her to honor her poets. You shall have the plaster bust on Monday.

1. William Winstanley, *The Lives of the Most Famous English Poets*, London, Samuel Manship, 1687, pp. 20–21. Miss Barrett made minor errors in copying the passage and omitted, probably accidentally, the bracketed words.

2. "O moral Gower, this book I directe / To thee" (*Troilus and Criseyde*, V,1856–1857).

3. Concerning the incestuous love of Canace for her brother and of Apollonius for his daughter, two of Gower's tales in *Confessio Amantis*, the Man of Law said, "Of swiche cursed stories I sey 'fy' ("Introduction to the Man of Law's Prologue," *The Canterbury Tales*, l. 80).

4. "Chaucer and Gower were to be spectators of the entrance of the Black Prince and King John of France into London" (Shackford, p. 57).

5. Sir Samuel Meyrick wrote to Haydon on February 7, 1843, "Gower would be twenty-seven years of age in 1357, and Chaucer about seventeen or eighteen, as on his legal examination as a witness in 1386 he states himself to be forty years and upwards" (*Correspondence*, I,437).

6. John Leland (1506?- 1552), antiquarian. His is the earliest known biography of Chaucer, included in his *Commentarii de Scriptoribus Britannicus*, first published in 1709 (Shackford, p. 58).

7. Nicholas Brigham (d. 1558), who built the tomb for Chaucer in Westminster Abbey.

8. Thomas Hoccleve or Occleve (1370?–1450?), author of *De Regimine Principium*, containing references to Chaucer's death.

9. These lines paraphrase a couplet from the original version of *Confessio Amantis* (ll. 2953*-2954*): "To sette an ende of alle his werk, / As he which is myn owne clerk" (Shackford, p. 59).

10. "The king of France, as he rode through London, was mounted on a white steed, with very rich furniture, and the prince of Wales on a little black hackney by his side" (Sir John Froissart, *Chronicles of England, France, Spain, and the Adjoining Countries*, tr. Thomas Johnes, New York, 1853, chapter 172, p. 110).

11. This was "probably Speght's edition; 1598, or 1602, or 1687, which contained a life of Chaucer" (Shackford, p. 59).

12. Richard Henry Horne's *Poems of Chaucer Modernized* (1841) contains Miss Barrett's translation of "Queen Annelida and False Arcite" and "The Complaint of Annelida to False Arcite," early versions of "The Knight's Tale."

13. "He semeth elvyssh by his contenance" (Prologue to "Chaucer's Tale of Thopas," *The Canterbury Tales*, 1. 13).

14. Miss Barrett probably referred to the eighteenth-century "Bodleian" portrait, which was not copied from the equestrian portrait of Chaucer in the Ellesmere manuscript, inherited by Lord Francis Egerton in 1833 from his father, Haydon's friend the Marquis of Stafford. The manuscript is now in the Huntington Library, San Marino, California (Shackford, pp. 60–61).

15. The unsigned review of *The Book of the Poets* in *The Athenaeum* of June 4, 1842 (pp. 497–499), contains many ideas expressed in this letter.

16. "The church (of the Augustinian priory of St. Mary Overie), burned in 1206 and rebuilt, was called *St. Saviour's* after 1540, when it became the parish church of Southwark and later Southwark Cathedral" (Shackford, p. 61).

# 22

*To Miss Barrett*
*February 19, 1843*

Sunday Night
Feb 19, 1843

My Sweetest Friend,

I send for your amusement pour se delasser, two porte-feuilles—one containing subjects for Painting, the other containing Sketches, heads, of Lords, Ladies, Men & Women, Whigs, Radicals, & Tories—which will amuse you.

I will send for them *Saturday*—only be careful in turning them over so they do not rub, and if you lift any up take them at *opposite* corners thus—[*a sketch*].

I am sure every trifle must be a relief, though your mind needs little but its own reflections to make it happy.

Do not let them out of your own apartment, & let no one handle them.

After all these precautions you will hardly think them worth the trouble of being careful.

The Cartoon gets on well—& I hope to have it soon done.

Curtius has had its share of abuse, as you have seen—It is not every one who can enter into its sentiment.

Are you on any work?—

I feel deeply for Mary Mitford, but fear at such a crisis, no increase of pension will be granted—nor do I anticipate great success in the scheme so heavy is the pressure on Rich & poor.

Her Father ought not for the gratification of his own indulgencies to have so left her. But it is no time to lament, one must exert oneself to help her—[1]

If she cant make 100 a year do in the Country, I am sure she will not be able to make it do in London—I am totally against her removal she is so unused to the savage nature of a London Literary life—

God bless you my dearest Friend & recover you with the Spring. May I be able occasionally to lighten the burthen of your captivity—

B. R. Haydon

*Address:* Miss B. Barrett / 50 Wimpole St.

1. *The Athenaeum* of February 18, 1843 (p. 146) contains a notice of a subscription to be raised for Miss Mitford to enable her to repay debts of between eight and nine hundred pounds incurred during her father's long and fatal illness.

# 23

## *To Haydon*
## *February 25, 1843* [1]

a writer, is of the nature of a personal interest; and I have heard from herself[2] that some four hundred & fifty pounds were collected for her during the first four days of the public appeal. As to her coming to London, although you say "no," I should say "yea,"—because I am selfish & have flattered myself into fancying that she might live here almost as cheaply, & in certain respects, *social* respects, more pleasantly. But her wishes are against it—and I am not *so* selfish as to struggle against the natural flow of them. For my own part, I pretend to be a poet—yet I like London. Chaucer said, "thys London whyche is to mee so dere and swete"[3]—& I can *almost* say it after him. I like to feel myself near to the great Heart, the "mighty Heart"[4] of the thinking people—to breathe this air full of consecrations from the Dead & living—and (not least) to have my green bag of new books regularly from the libraries. Otherwise you know, I might as well be in a wilderness—or a hermitage—or a convent—or a prison—as in this dark room, dark & silent, & from which the most extensive prospect presents a "prodigious grasp" — of chimney pots! —

Mr. Kenyon told me that he should take advantage of your kind offer about admitting him to the frescos. They are prospering I hope! — you are superior to east winds, & your "Daemon" is strong.

Which winds have shaken me of late — but I am writing, — altho' not a poem of any great length.[5]

Are you aware that the sonnet upon your picture of Wordsworth is in the American papers?[6] I must tell you of it.

Gratefully yours & truly

Elizabeth B Barrett

Here is a sketch of Anchises & Venus which suggests a most beautiful picture. Do tell me if you have painted it.[7] It is a comfort, — in the impertinence of the Athenaeum today; — that it admits the genius of Curtius, & the fineness of the worked out contrast of the animal terror & human devotedness.[8] And this (by proving that impertinent people may sometimes be right) encourages me to ask you why you called the Duke of Wellington's picture "C'est lui"? You who are so English, why should you not talk English? Was there a *reason* for the French? —

EBB

1. The first sheet of this letter is missing. It may be dated from the allusion to *The Athenaeum* of February 25, 1843 (see footnote 8).

2. Miss Mitford.

3. "This is from *The Testament of Love,* now attributed to Thomas Usk" (Shackford, p. 62).

4. Wordsworth, "Composed upon Westminster Bridge," l. 14.

5. The poem may have been "The Lost Bower" or "The Dead Pan" (Shackford, p. 62).

6. Miss Barrett was more popular in America at this time than in England. In a letter to Hugh Boyd, dated by John Kenyon "end of Jan. 1843," she wrote: "I send you the magazines which I have just received from America, and which contain, one of them, 'The Cry of the Human,' and the other, four of my sonnets. My correspondent tells me that the 'Cry' is considered there one of the most successful of my poems. . . . At page 343 of 'Graham's Magazine,' *Editor's Table,* is a review of me, which, however extravagant in its appreciation, will give your kindness pleasure. I confess to a good deal of pleasure

myself from these American courtesies, expressed not merely in the magazines, but in the newspapers; a heap of which has been sent to me by my correspondent – the 'New York Tribune,' 'The Union,' 'The Union Flag,' &c. – all scattered over with extracts from my books and benignant words about their writer. Among the extracts is the whole of the review of Wordsworth from the London 'Athenaeum,' an unconscious compliment, as they do not guess at the authorship" (*Letters*, I,120).

7. Haydon painted "Venus Appearing to Anchises" in 1826.

8. "Another odd piece of cabinet work [in the exhibition of the British Institution], bearing as odd a title – is Mr. Haydon's *C'est lui* (173): for who could imagine that these two French words designate the portrait of the Duke of Wellington? or rather of the Duke's back? . . . Mr. Haydon's 'daemon,' we fear, is rarely under due control. There is hardly a visitor to the gallery, who will not smile at the huge *Curtius* (384) [10½ ft. by 7½]. Yet there is genius in the picture: though the attitude of the horse resembles the coiling of an heraldic wyvern rather than the plunging of a steed, though the man wears on his brow the look of true opera heroism – and though the gulph be far more like the lonely rift of some desert moor, than the one which yawned in the Forum, its horror enhanced by contrast with the towers and temples, at whose very feet that fatal chasm unclosed – the contrast between animal terror and human devotedness is forcibly and finely rendered" (*The Athenaeum*, February 25, 1843, p. 195).


# 24

## To Miss Barrett
## February 27, 1843


London Feby 27th 1843

My dearest Friend,

Why did I put C'est lui? – for something of the same reason Alcibiades cut off his Dog's tail – for fun.[1]

I daresay my folies are a bore. The Venus & Anchises I painted for the late Lord de Tabley[2] – & Lady de Tabley liked it so much she made him will it to her, she has it now, and I believe it to be one of the prettiest things I ever did – a true Cytherea.

On dit, I could not make the Duke as well known as Napoleon by his back & a bit of his face. I betted I could, & not even show his face – & I have won –

The Athenaeum is impertinent enough but it is quite genteel in comparison with the Spectator which is scurrilous in the extreme.[3]

Nothing shows the lamentable state of the Critics [more] than their abuse of this Picture—so far from being huge, it is not bigger than a whole length Portrait, nor yet so big as Lawrence's George IV, and yet contrasted with the paltry things about it, it looks gigantic.

So they said of my Duke, but it is all a decepted [*deceptive*] View. The Duke was the exact height & so was his Horse—it is the mode & manner of selecting the essential from the superfluous which gives my figures an air of size—I measured Lawrence's George IV & it was 7 feet 6 inches high—& yet looked like a *small* Dandy from the reverse principle—

I was delighted to hear the success of your beautiful Sonnet—

I love Dogs,[4] but Newfoundlanders & Blood Hounds, which I can't keep—Mary Mitford once gave me a brace of Greyhounds—superb beauties—

I am happy to hear of her success, still I shall never be reconciled to her leaving her flowers, & cottage. It will destroy the poetry about her to have her in Society here.

I have overworked myself & am far from well—take care of yourself for the Summer. I shall send for the folios, positively Saturday next—

Ever yours faithfully,
B. R. Haydon

*Address:* Miss B Barrett / 50 Wimpole St.
*Postmark:* FE 27 1843

1. "Alcibiades had a dog which cost him seventy minas, and was a very large one, and very handsome. His tail, which was his principal ornament, he caused to be cut off, and his acquaintances exclaiming at him for it, and telling him that all Athens was sorry for the dog, and cried out upon him for this action, he laughed, and said, 'Just what I wanted has happened then. I wished the Athenians to talk about this, that they might not say something worse of me'" (Plutarch, *The Lives of the Noble Grecians and Romans,* tr. John Dryden, New York, The Modern Library, n.d., p. 238).

2. The first Baron de Tabley, formerly Sir John Fleming Leicester (1762–1827), art patron, who purchased "Venus Appearing to Anchises" in 1826 for £210. The picture is now owned by S. A. Oliver, Esq., Egham, Surrey.

3. "Haydon's *Curtius* (384) is a bold design, vigorously executed, but utterly deficient in dignity and elevated sentiment. The hero, who has just taken the fatal plunge into the abyss that yawns beneath, looks round with the assured self-complacency of an expert rider performing a daring feat of horsemanship. Not a trace of the noble character and lofty purpose of the patriotic Roman is visible in this florid, chubby-cheeked physiognomy; the vainglorious expression of which dissipates any idea of its owner being animated by sublime self-devotion. . . . What Mr. Haydon means by his scarecrow on two pegs, with its back towards you, which he entitles *C'est lui* (173), one may guess by the mounds of Waterloo amongst which it is stuck up; but the figure is no more characteristic of the Duke of Wellington than of any other man" (*The Spectator,* February 11, 1843, p. 139).

4. See Letter 99.

# 25

---

## *To Miss Barrett*
## *March 3, 1843*

London March 3 1843

You good for nothing—Painting the Poetry of surface & location!—Go along with you—I'll make Flush bark at ye. I say it is not—Painting is the art of conveying *thought* by the imitation of *things*—the *minds* are the same, you little Invisible, the means are different—I'll send you my lecture[1] if you don't behave well—I like you dealing out your anathemas from your sacred solitude, & your dog wagging his tail for joy at your mischief.

I swear if Mary Mitford comes to Town, she shall change her name! I'll call her Mary *Mud*ford—There is no fear Devonshire will do for her!

Know Caroline Norton![2]—to be sure I *did!* splendid Creature—I know her better than anybody ever did—& she knew me—I painted her as Cassandra for the Duke of Sutherland,[3] & mean to put her in several pictures.

The terrific power of her eye is not to be imagined—she was to be pitied deeply—she loved Vernon Smith's Brother,[4] who died of a fever, and she married an Ass to get rid of her pang![5]

She disturbed our domestic happiness & that my sweetest Mary[6] did not deserve,—she was talented, silly, overbearing, impassioned, vain, malicious, grand, ambitious, a heroine!—in civilized life she was thrown away! she should have been mistress to Tamerlane or Attila, she is a grand creature & had a mysterious power on my imagination! & has now—

To no one but you did I ever say this & do you say it to none—

Lady Seymour[7] was a love, a Venus in figure but no music in her Soul—not regularly handsome, cheeks too fat,—eyes too large—face too round, yet bewitching & fascinating, apathetic yet witty—her skin polished, her lips pouting, her figure perfect—Lady Dufferin[8] had more grace than either, was a most enchanting creature, great talent, & yet not masculine, well read, & yet not obtrusive—Indeed the 3 Sisters were at one time the most delightful Creatures I ever saw, I could have passed days with them, sketching, laughing, & intellectualizing, then they loved Genius, I flattered myself I was one—& you may imagine the rest—but they were so harrassed by Fashion & Society they thought they could dare its censures, the *abduction* ruined them, as it was called—but they were perfectly innocent, they had been insulted, & like Women of Spirit made old General repent.

This is a slight sketch of 3 of the loveliest Women I ever knew—though not one was as regular a beauty as Mary—I will send the Miniatures of Mary & my Mother, & you shall judge—I made sketches of all [of] them repeatedly—& remember their delightful Beauty, wit, & mischief, often—

Good night—I have just done a page looking with touching interest at the King John, & steamed him—you will like him—Chaucer is in in style [*a sketch of Chaucer and Gower*].

Adieu, but not for ever[9]—Have the Portfolios tied up if con-

venient & I will exchange them; would you like the anatomy
of Lion & Man?

Yours ever<br>B. R. Haydon

*Address:* Miss B. Barrett / 50 Wimpole St.
*Postmark:* MR 4 1843

1. The first volume of Haydon's *Lectures on Painting and Design* was
not published until 1844. He quotes from the first of these lectures, delivered
at the Mechanics' Institution on September 9, 1835: "Coleridge said painting
was a something between a thought and a thing. This is not enough. Painting is the art of conveying thoughts by the imitation of things" (*Lectures,* I,7).
2. The Hon. Mrs. Caroline Sheridan Norton (1808–1877), author and re-
nowned beauty. Haydon was infatuated with her for several years after their
meeting in 1833. In 1836 she separated from her husband, the Hon. George
Chapple Norton, who unsuccessfully sued for divorce, naming Lord Melbourne, the Prime Minister, as corespondent.
3. "Cassandra Predicting the Murder of Agamemnon" was painted in
1834. The Duke of Sutherland purchased it for £420.
4. Robert Vernon Smith's father, Robert Percy Smith, made a fortune in
India. "He lost a son and a daughter in their prime of youth, each of most
rare promise" (*The Annual Register, 1845,* "Chronicle," p. 259).
5. On June 30, 1827, Caroline Sheridan married Norton, brother and at
that time heir to the third Baron Grantley.
6. Haydon married a widow, Mrs. Mary Cawrse Hyman, on October 10,
1821. She survived him, dying in 1854.
7. Lady Seymour (1809–1884), sister of the Hon. Mrs. Norton. Her husband later became twelfth Duke of Somerset.
8. The Countess of Dufferin (1807–1867), another sister of the Hon.
Mrs. Norton. When Haydon knew her, her husband, Captain Price Blackwood, had not yet been raised to the peerage.
9. Byron, "Fare thee well," ll. 1–2. "Fare thee well! and if for ever, / Still
for ever, fare *thee well.*"

# 26

---

## *To Miss Barrett*
## *March 6, 1843*

*You* shall have a little note now—I fear you will think you
have got into a nice concern by honoring me with your beautiful Sonnet![1]—now do not you think so?

Will you tell me by return—the age of Gower & Chaucer at the time of the entry—

Was Chaucer 19—& was Gower 45?[2]

I went to St. Mary Overies yesterday & was quite delighted —you have inoculated me to see something in what is not Greek—

[*A sketch of Chaucer and Gower.*] That's the way they stand.

*Address:* Miss B. Barrett / 50 Wimpole St.
*Postmark:* MR 6 1843

1. Her "Sonnet on Haydon's Picture of Mr. Wordsworth" (see Letter 2, note 3).
2. Chaucer was born about 1340 and Gower about 1325. The former was therefore about seventeen and the latter about thirty-two at the time of the Black Prince's return from France to London in 1357.

# 27

## To Haydon
## March 6, 1843

6. March 1843

After the Battle of Poitiers, my dear Mr. Haydon, in the September of 1356, Froissart tells us that the Black Prince spent the whole winter at Bordeaux with his royal captive;[1] & thus, the entrance into London could not have taken place before the spring of 1357. Now, supposing Chaucer to have been born in 1328 (and the highest literary authorities certainly do suppose it)[2] this would bring him to his *29th* year at the period of the entrance. *I* believe that he was twenty-nine —but if Sir Samuel Meyrick & you determine it otherwise, you must alter Gower's received age to suit Chaucer's—there being a seniority on the part of Gower, of probably some four or five years. Chaucer's fatherhood in English poetry was not won from his contemporary by a seniority, – but by writing English poems before his friend did – altho' Gower's Confessio Amantis (his only English work) did appear before Chaucer's *chief* work, the Canterbury Tales. Chaucer died in 1400 – and his fellow-poet survived him two years.[3]

The more I think of that signature which is said to throw back the age, the greater are my misgivings. If Chaucer was only 19 in 1357, dying in 1400 he could only be 62 – and yet there are testimonies to his dying at an advanced age. Why Gower at the close of his *Confessio amantis* places in the mouth of the Lady Venus a recommendation to Chaucer to "put an ende of al his werke"[4] *on account of his age – & after that* Chaucer had time to write his voluminous Canterbury Tales & die! – Could he have died at sixty two only?

Well! – I have a great respect for Sir Samuel Meyrick – & a great misgiving about the signature! – There is the truth of it.

And the matter of fact is, – that if you make Chaucer nineteen you must make Gower twenty three or four. But Warton,[5] Godwin, Sir Egerton Brydges,[6] would *not* make Chaucer nineteen, but twenty-nine.

My dear friend, you will scarcely know what to think of me for not replying more quickly to your two letters – but the east wind has been slaying me, – & I was too unwell yesterday to finish & send what I began to write. I accept your kindness eagerly about the lions &c. – & also in relation to the miniatures. – Able to guess at much beauty from certain sketches, I am interested in having the full vision completed by a sight of the finished likeness of Mrs. Haydon. Is it true by the [*the rest of the letter is missing*].

1. Jean Froissart, *Chronicles,* 2 vols., London, 1523–1525, chapter 168.
2. Later in this letter Miss Barrett refers to William Godwin (1756–1836), author of *The Life of Geoffrey Chaucer* (2 vols., London, 1803), who wrote: "The usual date assigned to the birth of Chaucer is 1328" (I,xxiv).
3. Gower died in 1408.
4. See Letter 21, note 9.
5. Thomas Warton (1728–1790), author of *The History of English Poetry*

*from the Close of the 11th to the Commencement of the 18th Century* (3 vols., London, 1774–1781), edited by Richard Price. Warton stated categorically that Chaucer was born in 1328 (rev. ed., 1840, London, II, 127).

6. Sir Samuel Egerton Brydges (1762–1837) was a "poet, editor, antiquarian, but not an authority on Chaucer. It seems probable that Miss Barrett had access to his *Censura Literaria,* 1809; *Restituta,* 1816; *British Bibliographer,* 1822, works found then in a gentleman's library. Miss Spurgeon's *Chaucer, Criticisms and Allusions,* Chaucer Society, specifies Brydge's allusions" (Shackford, pp. 64–65).

# 28

---

## *To Miss Barrett*
## *March 7, 1843*

*Confidential*                                                    London March 7, 1843
My dearest Friend,

I can believe that of Caroline Norton, but she met her match here, and was completely floored; what I admired so much was in Mary, her fearless determination to stand up for her own love & rights, and she did it like a Heroine; there was no cause for her uneasiness,[1] but she fancied it, it was fierce—the children took Mama's part, with such fury, that a fine bust I had of her when I was out they took down in the Court & beat it all to pieces—

*This is entirely confidential*—sometimes one longs to tell all sorts of things—and is afraid to open one's lips—She excited my imagination terrifically & nothing but my devoted love to one dear being saved my brain—but it was a terrific struggle, & I look back on it with terror—

You must know I never loved properly but once, and then I married—nor do I believe any one can love with equal intensity, twice.

Caroline Norton's eyes & air, & talents burdened me & I suffered agony at times, but the heartlessness of fashion is its own cure: still, I cannot bear the thought that even in thought, my allegiance was disturbed—*only* disturbed.

She had a hankering to disturb families, but she caught a Tartar here—*more hereafter* at which you will be *highly interested.*

Why you must be convinced I am the *quintessence of Vanity!*—My own head for Solomon & Curtius!—ay and Alexander the Great! and Dentatus![2] don't faint—you must know, you study your own head for Expression, and you will find chalk studies, but it is only as *a help*—Except in Curtius, for which my head is the best I ever saw, I have never made a Portrait—the sly malice of the Critics is exquisite—they pretended not to know it is myself, call it chubby cheeked, & a want of the heroic, & all sorts of things to reach me as if ignorant—

To illustrate the principle—I will tell you an anecdote—I had an old Servant & model, an old Life guardsman[3] who make the best servants in the World—I always rubbed in my Pictures from him, Man, Women & children, using him only to keep me right.[4] One day Lord Elgin called when I was out, and walked into the painting room. Salmon attended him, the Picture was the Christ entering Jerusalem, where I had a Penitent Girl, hiding her face, and ushered into Christ's presence by her anxious Mother—the whole was merely sketched in—Lord Elgin said who sat for that, & who sat for this & the old Soldier (bolt upright) as if on duty said to every question *I did—My Lord*—who sat for the Mother? said Lord Elgin—*I did my Lord said Salmon* (6 feet 3 high & heroic in figure)—and who sat for that beautiful Girl, *I did My Lord,* said Salmon, at which Lord Elgin burst into a fit of laughter & said, By heavens you are a useful Model!—

Lord Elgin was fond of a good story, & made the most of this, as you may imagine.

They abuse Curtius as if sitting too *low* in the Horse—mere trash; here is a section—[*a sketch showing the position of Curtius on the back of his horse*]. Put this in front—[*another sketch of Curtius*].[5]

I have done all but the Fool, which I do today – I mean to make him & John the only grave personages in the Cartoon – the one grave at the uncertainty of Fortune, the [other] grave at the blindness of human Triumph! [*A sketch of a human head, half of it revealing the skull.*] as I have seen in an old Print.

Have you read Madam d'Arblay – I hurt my eyes last night reading the article in the Edin[burgh] – it is excellent & I suspect Macaulay; have you seen his lays?[6] – or Eyre's narrative[7] – or Pressnitz on Water[8] – Mary is mad about it, & is drinking cold water like a Fish – which I have done all my life –

Oh you delicate creature does the East Wind touch you? I suppose I shall come to it –

God bless you – I'll send down two or more folios – as they seem to please you & then return the others – I shall be ever delighted & consider it a duty to relieve by trifles now & then your peculiar state, though your own mind is quite enough for its own solace.

Ever yours

B. R. Haydon

*Address:* Miss B. Barrett / 50 Wimpole St.
*Postmark:* MR 8 1843

1. Many entries in Haydon's diary for 1834 refute this statement. I own a small commonplace book kept by Mary Haydon at this period, which shows her utter misery at her husband's infatuation with Mrs. Norton and her sisters. For example, in an entry headed "Sunday, August 1834," she wrote: "I have passed another night of great suffering. Oh God, what will all this extreme pain of mind come to? Dear Benjamin has given me this book to put down my thoughts, as relief to feelings that can no longer contain themselves. . . . I ask for redress from the Almighty for the deep, deep misery I have suffered and suffered without cause."
2. The head of Jesus in Haydon's "Christ's Entry into Jerusalem" also bears a marked resemblance to the artist.
3. John Salmon or Sammons, a former corporal in the Horseguards. He was dead by 1836.
4. Many women in Haydon's pictures have very masculine arms and shoulders.
5. Haydon clarified his contention by two diagrams in the entry of March 13, 1843, in his diary. "The critics say Curtius is too low on his seat – the

noodles [*two diagrams of Curtius and his horse, lettered A and B*]. When the horse bends his neck, the nape [A] moves not. B is the seat, and this section explains it" (*Diary*, V,253).

6. Thomas Babington Macaulay (1800–1859) was the author of the review of the *Diary and Letters of Madame D'Arblay* in *The Edinburgh Review*, January 1843 (76,272–297). His *Lays of Ancient Rome* was first published in 1842.

7. Vincent Eyre's *The Military Operations at Cabul, which Ended in the Retreat and Destruction of the British Army* is reviewed in *The Edinburgh Review*, February 1843 77,139–146).

8. Vincenz Priessnitz (1801–1851), an Austrian farmer, originated the "water cure" or hydropathy. In 1843 in London Richard Beamish published *Approximate Rationale of the Cold Water Cure, as Practiced by Vincent Priessnitz.*

# 29

---

## *To Miss Barrett*
## *March 16, 1843*

London March 16, 1843

My dearest Friend,

I saw the Ecce Homo today, & there is very great merit in it—the expression is subdued without being heavy, the head carefully painted & correctly drawn & it is a work (if the artist be young) on which to calculate.

The faults are hardness, bad color & not elevated & refined character, but still it is of very great merit—the half tints are green instead of pearly—but your Friend may be proud of his protegé. I have got through both Cartoons [1] & now comes the relaxation of the String—I must be at something else.

Goodnight

B. R. Haydon

*Address:* Miss B. Barrett / 50 Wimpole St.
*Postmark:* MR 17 1843

1. "The Black Prince Entering London in Triumph" and "Adam and Eve." Both were shown at the Cartoon Exhibition held in Westminster Hall, June 1843.

# 30

*To Miss Barrett*
*March 22, 1843*

London March 22nd 1843

My dear Invisible Friend,

By this time you must be a compleat Artist after being admitted into the recesses of an Artist's mind—how he puts forth his thoughts & how he uses his models, & how he does every thing.

I have got through both Cartoons, & revised & finally corrected the great one—I revise & finally correct the Black Prince tomorrow, and then I "cast my bread upon the waters" [1] —Pray for my success!—

I have done my duty—and if I had not after all the uproar I had made on this very principle and after having made my Pupils begin it 24 years ago with so great a success that Goethe ordered a set of the Elgin drawings for his house at Weimar,[2] where they are now preserved for ever by purchase of Government—had I shrunk now, I should have been considered to have run away at the 11th hour after fighting the 10th.

But it is hard to descend into the arena for the prize I was entitled to 29 years ago at the conclusion of Solomon,[3] and though an old man (57) yet I am stronger in body & mind, by the blessing of God, than at that early age and more fit, by long experience & suffering, to do my Country honor.

Yet what chance have I?

The World of fashion are not moved by justice, but novelty! —Some young Tyro, who may make what the Ladies call a *nice* cartoon *so finished* is very likely to run away with *my* honors.

Nor are they likely to distinguish between the mere Cartoon drawn & the painter—the one making the Cartoon a means for an End, the other an end only, & as helpless on the Wall as a Baby.

*March 1843 / 49*

However I have done my duty as Nelson said, & I thank God for this great opportunity of doing it.

I trust my dearest Friend all I confided to you of C. N. is sacred especially to your own sex.

It is not quite fair of me, but I, in a moment of "abandon" forgot myself.

I hope Mary Mitford is quite at rest about her Father's debts —But I suspect to make us easy she fibs about the amount—Is it so?—

I shall want Wordsworth shortly but will send you another.

I am ever Thine affectionately,

B. R. Haydon

*Address:* Miss B. Barrett / 50 Welbeck St. (The words "Try Wimpole St. Not known as Directed" have been added in another hand.)
*Postmark:* MR 23 1843

1. Ecclesiastes 11:1.
2. Goethe owned cartoons of the Elgin Marbles (originally known as "The Fates" and "Theseus," but now entitled "Aphrodite and Dione" and "Dionysus") made by Charles Landseer and William Bewick. His house in Weimar became the Goethe Nationalmuseum, where the cartoons are still hung.
3. "The Judgment of Solomon" was completed in April 1814 and purchased by Sir William Elford and J. W. Tingcombe for £735 (*Diary*, V,588).

# 31

## *To Miss Barrett*
## *March 24, 1843*

My dearest Friend,

You mistake my studies for future use—for relics—nothing of the sort—they are measured essentials of the Duke's figure.

You think higher of Napoleon than the Duke—I do not—my reasons are Napoleon with the resources of Europe gained a Throne, & so mismanaged them he lost it.

Wellington (a subject) with most limited resources, first beat all his Marshalls & then himself.

An ounce of morality & honor is worth a lb. of Genius.

560 Officers of Napoleon's broke their parole in one year, and were welcomed by Napoleon; 7 I believe of ours did so & were *sent back* – the result of such a system could be foreseen.

Perhaps you were not born – I have no time I will go into the whole thing for you, with *all my Soul* –

I thank God I was always a believer in the Duke from the moment he gave up the Irish Secretaryship[1] nearly 7000 a year because it interfered with his military pursuits! – that's a *Great Genius* said I – I believed in him for ever –

I reviewed the Manuscrit venu de St. Helene[2] and did *him* Glory – in alluding to Napoleon I predicted all that happened & when Napoleon stamped his foot on the shore at Cannes & said "Voila le congrès dessous"[3] I *said* – it is – for you are but an instrument for the greater glory of my hero – Leigh Hunt laughed – I said wait it will only be a working up for Wellington –

After the Battle of Waterloo, I called on Hunt – & fought him & Hazlitt & beat 'em for two hours on the *relative* Military skill – & I mean to write an article in U. S. Gazette on this battle,[4] which you shall see.

Lord Fitzroy[5] has seen it & says it is the strongest thing & best put he has seen – he told me so.

I venerate the Hero, as De Stael says, coming down to the House of Commons without a *single attendant* – uncovering his grand head, & receiving the thanks of the Speaker! – no drum – no trumpet – no cannon – no imposture.

I'll wish ye well now you have roused my Wellingtonian Fury – God Bless ye & may you survive it.

B. R. H.

*Address:* Miss B. Barrett / 50 Wimpole Street
*Postmark:* MR 24 1843

1. Wellington (at that time Sir Arthur Wellesley) accepted the post of Chief Secretary for Ireland on the formation of a new cabinet by the Duke of Portland, March 25, 1807 (Herbert Maxwell, *The Life of Wellington*, London, 1899, I,81). J. W. Croker served as deputy-secretary when Wellington left England in June 1808 to assume command of the allied forces in Portugal (*ibid.*, I,97).

2. *Manuscrit venu de St. Hélène, d'une manière inconnue*, London, J. Murray, 1817. This spurious autobiography of Napoleon was written by J. F. Lullin de Chateauvieux. Haydon expressed his opinion that the book was authentic in the *Examiner* of April 27 and May 4, 1817, pp. 262–263 and 275–276.

3. On escaping from Elba, Napoleon landed near Antibes on March 1, 1815. He passed through Cannes on his way to Paris, and there expressed his contempt for the Congress of Vienna, whose deliberations were suspended during the Hundred Days.

4. Haydon wrote in his diary for January 14, 1844. "Wrote a capital letter in defence of the battle of Waterloo & sent it to United Service Journal." The letter appeared in *Colburn's United Service Magazine*, February 1844 (44,279–281). Haydon defended Wellington against detractors who argued that luck rather than military genius won the Battle of Waterloo.

5. Lord Fitzroy Henry Somerset, later Baron Raglan (1788–1855), aide-de-camp to Wellington at Waterloo, where he was wounded.

# 32

## *To Miss Barrett*
## *March 28, 1843*

London March 28 1843

Consider the genius opposed to Wellington, & the poverty of talent opposed to Napoleon[1] — Wellington had no Beaulieu's, Melas', & Wurmsers to fight but Soults, & Massenas, & Junots, & Marmonts, & all the men who had risen by their Genius from the ranks. Napoleon was never fairly opposed – & when he was – he was beaten – Acre & Waterloo.

No words can do justice to that energy of mind, that patient reliance, that inspired confidence, that modest unboasting foresight, with which he opposed, thwarted, & drove before him Massena at Torres Vedras — you must be too young to recollect, his first appearance — never shall I forget my wonder at his crossing the Mondego & taking up a position in *front* of the French!

At Paris 1815—Sir Walter said to the Duke, "Suppose Blucher had not come up"—"I could have kept my ground till next day," was his reply—"Granting you had been obliged to fall back" —"I could have kept all the armies of Europe at bay in Soignies"—"Suppose Grouchy had come first"— "Blucher was close behind him, & *we* would not have left Napoleon an army next day"—These are word for word— the words of the Duke—from Sir Walter to me—

I met Lord Hill at Lord Palmerston's 1833—he lived at West-bourne house & he put me down, as my house was on the road —finding myself alone with him in the carriage—I said, "Was there ever a time at Waterloo your Lordship desponded?" [2] "Desponded," said he, "never a moment—there was no panic, we were in advance towards the afternoon—no rear guard was formed—I never had any doubt. To Halle on the *right,* a strong division was sent—to guard against surprise. To Ohain [3] on the left, another was placed to be ready for Blucher. Neither of these was moved all day till the pursuit—and the first thing (*if in danger*) would have been the movement of these divisions to form a rear guard."

"When Blucher arrived—had a single regiment been broken?"—"No"—"Were we not in advance in the morning?" "Yes—Buonaparte said our Centre was forced because La Haye Sainte was taken but La Haye Sainte was *not our centre* but a farm 100 yards in front"—"and did he keep it?"—"No—he was driven out." "When Desaix arrived at Marengo from Novi [Ligure], he found Napoleon with one wing ruined—& in full change of position. Did Blucher find the Duke so?"—"Blucher was a part of the Duke's force as Desaix was [of] Napoleon's, and it is perfectly absurd to say the Duke owes his safety to Blucher, any more than that he owed his safety to British troops—Blucher was a part of his combination, and all that Blucher did was to perform his portion & complete the destruction the Duke had prepared for him."

Napoleon said the Duke shewed no genius because he fought the battle with one defile in his rear—but what Genius did Napoleon shew who fought it with *three* defiles in his rear.[4] The fact is Napoleon was *forced* to fight where the Duke chose, & was fairly & honestly & compleatly beaten.

Now am I not justified in my adoration of Wellington?

You will be quite a General after this lecture.

Ever yours,

B. R. Haydon

*Address:* Miss B. Barrett / 50 Wimpole St.
*Postmark:* MR 29 1843

1. Haydon thus refers to three Austrian generals who lost significant battles to Napoleon and to four French generals who won important engagements for him.
2. Haydon recorded his conversation with Major-General Viscount Hill (1772–1842) in his diary, October 17, 1833.
3. Halle (or Hal) is a village about eight miles west of Waterloo and Ohain is located about four miles to the southeast.
4. As Haydon noted in his diary, June 30, 1840, these defiles were Carleroi, Gemappe, and Quatre-Bras.

# 33

---

## *To Miss Barrett*
## *March 31, 1843*

London, March 31, 1843

Ah, My dear Friend,

Here's the rub—why was he crowned? Why did he rising from sub Lieutenant, to wield a great Nation, why did *he* disgrace himself by such folly? This was the wretched weakness of *his* mind—he did not feel the naked Majesty of Genius.

Think of Napoleon, the first day he went to Chapel, an Emperor, putting his hand to his forehead in a White glove, because it was the etiquette of Louis XIV!!!—Bourienne says they all watched to see if he would do it—& to their infinite amusement he did it—what weakness. Think of Napoleon jumping for joy when Duroc *dined with the King of Prussia!*

Napoleon crowning himself & Caesar passing the Rubicon, from them to be lesser Men than Wellington, who would perish at the stake rather than do either.

I admit it may be said, that showing Europe the power to crown himself, exhibited the greatness of Genius—but he should have dashed the Crown from him, & remained the Napoleon who could do these things—& do without them too.

I am by birth a Constitutional Monarchist, but that does not prevent me from glorying in a Man proving the impotency of Station. Consider the deep injury he did to the cause of Genius by his treachery; consider the glory he might have conferred on it, consider the blow he gave it, which it won't recover for 100 years if then—Consider the great moment he lost—& Why?—because he wanted to play King!! Oh Napoleon, when I look at your Bust, I could knock it in a thousand pieces & stamp it to powder!

Contrast this, with the simple, upright, honorable, Manly moral duty of Wellington's mind—The greatest Geniuses are those, where the basis is common sense—Can any thing be more beautiful than the common sense of Shakespeare & Homer, Raffael & Titian, Newton & Socrates. Was there any common sense in making a staunch Friend like Spain, an exasperated Enemy? Was there any common sense in proudly trying to do in one Campaign, what from the physical nature of the Country could only be done in two? Was there any thing like the commonest sense of the commonest Understanding in making an enemy of the Pope, getting into a quarrel where Religious prejudices were sure to beat him.

After Crowning, Spain, Russia & the Pope, were the three great political cancers of his career; & they were his ruin.

Most men can manage Adversity, but it requires the greatest Understanding to regulate Success—In this I think he was deficient—Wellington has proved his Understanding adequate to both.

Depend on it Napoleon rose by his Genius not being competently opposed at beginning; from the moment he was competently opposed he declined—What is the merit due to him who had the foresight to see he could be opposed, who did oppose, & ultimately destroy him with resources, so limited they are laughable, a Government so ignorant of his merit that they eternally thwarted him & officers so little confident in him or themselves that he had more trouble to regulate their minds to obedience than beat the enemy.

The Duke never suffers his imagination to controul his reason or touch his heart.

Napoleon was often the Victim of the one & the other. The Duke may not be agreable to the fancy, but he reaches the understanding.

In private life I know Wellington to be a simple & delightful person,[1] I know he has none of the meanesses which Bourienne & the Duchesse [d'Abrantes] describe of Napoleon; he is fond of children, he romps, dances, laughs, plays with them—he tells a story better than Sir Walter Scott, he is charitable & liberal in his charities, he is not revengeful but forgiving, he looks on life as a long struggle of Duty, & he has made it so,—duty to his Country, his Government & his God—For any purpose military, or political, would he have told a falsehood? For every purpose in the one or the other, would Napoleon have hesitated?—Wherein was Wellington Bloody & cruel, Wherein has he ever been treacherous & mean? Imagine Napoleon & Wellington before *their God*, Napoleon might & perhaps will defy him, Wellington will await his decision, and on a principle of moral duty submit to his will. That's the touch-stone after all of what is *truly* Great. As to his dying on a rock, I say to you, & to all not alive at the Time—you can never estimate the feeling of the World existing in his Time. I admit his romantic, "Je viens comme Themistocle" &c. &c. was too high a touch for the Court of George IV[2]—I admit he might have been allowed to live here, but consider the morbid nature of democracy, generally the result of Fog & indigestion, consider the delight Men have to annoy, the Authorities they must obey, – consider the tool the Whigs & Radicals would have made of him, and then say if security of his Person ought to have been the first thought.

His word he never regarded – His honor he sneered at – He had lost perception of Truth, he lied so regularly to conceal it, he believed at last what he knew to be untrue – To conclude more injury would have accrued to Liberty & thought by the success of Napoleon, than good, & it was a useful lesson to Nations, when a Great Genius who rose on the Shoulders of Liberty, died on a rock for Betraying her – Lay this to your heart & farewell.[3]

B. R. Haydon

I am delighted you like dear Mary's face. It was perfect – a Vision – Eve would have been jealous & Venus got in a rage – I painted her as Venus coming to Anchises from Homer's hymn which Lady de Tabley made Lord de Tabley *will* to her,[4] & she has it now. My dear Mother was a grand head.

*Address:* Miss B. Barrett / 50 Wimpole St.
*Postmark:* AP 1 1843

1. The Duke of Wellington cordially entertained Haydon as a guest for three days at Walmer Castle in October 1839 while he sat for the portrait now at Apsley House.

2. On July 14, 1815, before being sent to St. Helena, Napoleon wrote as follows to the Prince Regent, later George IV: "Altesse Royale, en butte aux factions qui divisent mon pays et à l'inimitié des puissances de l'Europe, j'ai terminé ma carrière politique, et je viens, comme Thémistocle, m'asseoir au foyer du peuple britannique. Je me mets sous la protection de ses lois, que je réclame de Votre Altesse Royale, comme du plus puissant, du plus constant et du plus généreux de mes ennemis." (Your Royal Highness, in the midst of factions which have rent my country and the enmity of the European powers, I have closed my political career, and I come like Themistocles to throw myself on the mercy of the British people. I seek the protection of their laws, which I am asking of your Royal Highness as the most powerful, the most faithful and the most generous of my enemies. *Correspondence de Napoleon Ier,* Paris, 1869, 28,301.)

In spite of his leadership in the Athenian naval victory over the Persians at Salamis, Themistocles was later exiled. He ultimately went to Persia, where he received a pension from King Artaxerxes I, son of Xerxes, the loser at Salamis.

3. *Macbeth,* I,v,15. "Lay it to thy heart, and farewell."

4. Haydon referred to his picture "Venus Appearing to Anchises," painted in 1826 and purchased by Sir John Leicester, later first Baron de Tabley. The picture was inspired by Homeric Hymn III, "To Aphrodite," describing the goddess' love for the mortal Anchises.

# 34

## To Miss Barrett
## April 2, 1843

London April 2, 1843

The Rock melancholy! but it was poetical! It surrounded his latter days with a halo of Romance, that dying on the Throne never could have given! — Besides it was just though cruel, it was that even handed justice, which held the poisoned chalice to his own lips[1] & made him drink the dregs, as he had made poor Toussaint do before! — there was nothing Napoleon in the wantonness of power inflicted on others, was not in the end inflicted on himself.

Security of his person was the first object after 25 years [of] war — his word of honor was nothing — his genius, everything — if he fretted against his bars, what was to be done — if he refused consolation, it could not be forced; suppose he had come to England, when the morbidity of democrats & the hatred all men feel at being obliged to submit to a Government at all, would have made him a very convenient handle to torment the powers that be;[2] it was a very extraordinary dilemma, for which the mind of the Foreign Secretary[3] was not fit, & there was not poetry enough in any Minister to relish or enter into Napoleon's allusion to Themistocles! — Do you, *can* you believe his sudden change from deep rooted hatred of England, to manly candour of submission, was honest? — you cannot — By remaining here he would have soon had a party of ardent *jeune* England, & all the discontented would have made him a bye word & rallying point & focus of opposition —

I never can believe that so good a man as Lord Liverpool, or so upright a Man as the Duke had any motive in sending him to St. Helena, than security. £20,000 was spent in sending him out every comfort on Earth, on a fit out, for I saw the greater part of the Articles, but if he got sulky & proud & captious & irritable, these things were not intended – At the very time he was affecting to be poor & broke up his plate to sell, Gorgeaux[4] told Lord Bathurst (I believe it was him) he Napoleon had 10,000 Napoleons in his chest.

The fact is, My dearest Friend, he found himself *compelled* to surrender as a finesse to escape being made a Prisoner of War – whether the Government were justified in taking advantage of his surrender in the way they [did] is a nice question of honor, but what would the Nations of Europe have said if they had let him go, on such a principle especially one too who never regarded any principle, where his policy or ambition were concerned – Posterity must decide – but I know, if I had suffered such anxiety for years as all the Governments of Europe had suffered, from this Man's genius, I would not have [been] *very* scrupulous as to keeping him, when once in my power.

With respect to the private characters of the Duke & Napoleon, can they be compared? – During the Duke's absence in India, old Lord Mulgrave told me some disease so affected the Woman he was engaged to that she released the Duke from his engagement – he said – no – he would keep it – & he did – Would he have divorced Josephine? In comparing Henry VIII with Napoleon, of course Napoleon shines – in *this* case – but was it noble to lacerate the Woman's heart, who had loved him when he was poor, & shared his Throne & Crown when he was rich? & for what – a thick-lipped – thick hearted – thick headed Austrian! would Josephine have left him like Lady Byron at the moment his household Gods were shivered on the hearth? – not she – he should have married a Russian Princess, that was the mistake, said Lord John Russell when he was sitting to me, no said I, he should have married a fine French Woman, My Lord, this shocked a *leetle* his aristocracy, and he hesitated out, yes indeed, *or* a fine French Woman![5] But in his heart he cursed me for saying it before him.

Napoleon threw the cause of Genius 100 years back, the good he did was accidental, the Evil certain; – the Whigs stuck to him, because they looked on him as the representative of the Great Cause, let him do what he would. Despot or not, it was no matter, the fact, that *there he* was, a Sous lieutenant of Artillery on the Throne of the greatest Country on the Continent was evidence of the success of the Cause – I say no – It is an injury to have *him* remain as representative of that Cause, that glorious cause, who has betrayed in the remotest way one iota of the professed principles of that Cause – & therefore I gloried in his ruin – Hazlitt & I, decadent Tories, used to fight it out till his lips got blue with rage – but he never could answer the above – Did he, or did he not, betray the cause? – he did, but the fact of his dying on the Throne, would have been a glory & a good, the evil would have died with him, the good remained[6] – let it both perish, I used to say, if such a character be its pillar! –

I used to maintain less injury would accrue to the cause of liberty in France by the return of the Bourbons than by the permanence of Napoleon, & has it not been so?? Posterity can never properly estimate the state of the World's feeling about that Man while he was living. I remembered him from 1796 & never lost sight of him, I visited his haunts within 3 weeks after his abdication,[7] saw the extinguisher on the last candle he read by, at Fontainbleau, the ashes in his grate, the Volume of Hume he had been reading! – staid 14 days at the Palace there, went on parade, got acquainted with officers & men of his guard, heard the Crash of his terrific band of drums, at 9 o'Clock in the warm Summer evenings, as I lay musing in his Jardin Anglais, with his little Column built against the setting sun, topped by a Golden Eagle grappling the Earth! I sketched his bed, his column, his Garden, I doated on his Genius, saw his Salon de repos, & staid in it musing – where none went but the Empress – touched

Marie Louise's piano, & made it strike out an harmonious tone! found the King of Rome's play things at Rambouillet, just as he had left, when hurried away, with his Mother [and] the Dutchess of Montebello. In fact I dreamt away half a Summer, forgot the Louvre & the Transfiguration – the Cossacs & the Allies and drank deep of all those great emotions which crowd the heart & Brain, at the sudden hurling down a grand Military Hero, when one stands on the very heart he has hallowed by his gigantic tread.

If I can find my 3 letters on Paris I published 1814[8] – I will send them to you – I write this Sunday evening, put them both in the fire – & believe me ever your affectionate fr.

B. R. Haydon

*Address:* Miss B. Barrett / 50 Wimpole St.
*Postmark:* AP 3 1843

1. *Macbeth,* II,i,10–12. "This even-handed justice / Commends th' ingredients of our poison'd chalice / To our own lips."
2. Romans 13:1.
3. Viscount Castlereagh (1769–1822), later second Marquis of Londonderry, was foreign secretary in Lord Liverpool's cabinet when Napoleon wrote to the Prince Regent.
4. General Baron Gaspar Gourgaud (1783–1852) accompanied Napoleon to St. Helena. He went to England in 1818 to testify before government officials concerning conditions there. The third Earl Bathurst (1762–1834), secretary for war and colonies, wrote: "General Gourgaud stated himself to have been aware of General Buonaparte having received a considerable sum of money in Spanish doubloons, viz. £10,000, at the very time he disposed of his plate" (Walter Scott, *The Life of Napoleon Buonaparte,* Philadelphia, 1827, III,318).
5. Haydon's conversation with Lord John Russell took place on November 2, 1832 (*Diary,* III,659–660).
6. *Julius Caesar,* III,ii,80–81. "The evil that men do lives after them, / The good is oft interred with their bones."
7. Napoleon abdicated on April 11, 1814, and was banished to Elba. Haydon and Wilkie went to France on May 26, 1814, visiting Dieppe, Rouen, Paris, Fontainebleau, and many other places associated with Napoleon. Haydon remained in France until July 17 (*Diary,* I,352–382).
8. The letters appeared in the *Examiner,* August 22, August 29, and September 5, 1814, signed "E. S." (for "English Student," a pseudonym frequently used by Haydon).

# 35

---

*To Miss Barrett*
*April 3, 1843*

London April 3rd 1843

There never was a more desperate and daring attempt to enslave the intellectuality of Man than that made by Napoleon—nothing holy—nothing sacred—but he wielded to make available to his desire! I saw in Notre Dame round a statue of Jesus Christ, at the points of the golden Glory N.N.N. in gold letters—N.N.N. glittered outside & inside Palaces & Halls—Altars & Churches; you felt haunted by his influence, the Eternal N.N.N. pursued your imagination, it mingled in prayer, in confession, in the innocence of the baptismal sprinkling, or the last awful ceremony of Death! Napoleon determined to master the human will, & began at the earliest period of human perception, the budding boy— Did you ever see his Catechism? "I believe Napoleon to be an engine of God" &c. &c. &c.[1]

You were a Baby or not born, you see now only the Romance, the mystery, the heroism, the daring, the Grandeur, the Eclat of his Life—as [I] saw & felt & remember all its power, & terror, and diabolism, his mysterious murders, his hideous and iron vigor, his heartless despotism!—his wanton dishonor!

Ah, my sweetest Friend, you do not know what the World escaped!—I do—An old Aide camp of his Russian Campaign said he wanted to establish a new Religion & I believe it— he was going to work when he was checked.

Jamais la Providence ne planait si proche de la terre, I think Madam de Stael said—it is not to be questioned—the Winter set in a Month earlier than the oldest Russian ever remembered, and was the severest ever known—this I had from my Uncle Mordwinoff[2] a Russian, who married my dear Mother's Sister.

You should have seen Paris, that City of splendor & blood & Cotillon in 1814 — you should have seen, as I saw but which as a Woman you never could see, the Palais Royal at midnight, with the fragments of his officers, reckless, sacrilegious, blasphemous, abandoned Youths, seeking for revenge, & vicious & debauched from spite & mortification — longing for blood & to murder something or somebody to regain their self Estimation! You should have heard them shout

Vive Napoleon
Vive ce grand conquerant,
Ce diable de Napoleon
A beaucoup plus de talent
Que votre Henry quatre
Et tous ses descendans.

You should as I did have followed them to the gambling tables, theatres, & streets, got into talk, praise Napoleon, swear *they* were never beaten, but toujours trahis! — you should have shared their confidences, extracted their secrets, their hopes, their desires, their passions — you should have done all this before you could judge Napoleon — I did all this, I have cursed him, & his heartless power, so to eradicate, so to corrupt, so to destroy for ever (for the age of education was past) the feelings, the purity, & the Minds of the Youth of so great a Country.

It is all very fine to read Madame la Duchesse & think him tres aimable & De Stael said Napoleon was a system not a Man, I say the Duke & he were two systems; it was only necessary for a collision to take place for one to destroy the other — You never saw the Napoleon I painted for Sir Robert Peel — musing at St. Helena — I will lend it to you — the origin of Wordsworth's sublime sonnet.[3] It was a melancholy & awful sight to watch his Officers, they looked like the cinders of an extinct Volcano, — black, dingy, & fierce! — Their native politeness never forsook them to me, & I have had long, touching, & romantic Conversations with them.

The morning the Russians were breaking up from the

Champs Elisées, an old Marengo Officer, with one leg, came up to me, — he shook his head & pointed to the destruction of the trunks of the Trees, the ruin of the Walls, the filth of the relics they had left behind! — We did not speak for a little time, when I said, "Depuis quand avez vous perdu cette affaire?" pointing to his leg — the old Moustache turned round, & said with fierce pride, "à Marengo! Monsieur" — we were then silent & he turned again as the Russians were filing away — "Ah — Why did he go so far?"

I visited the whole field of Battle of Paris, on entering a large Gentleman's House at Pantin, I walked right into the Parlour, one old Butler was sweeping out the dung of the Cossacs' Horses who had been bivouacked in the parlor, a hole being cut in the floor & stakes driven in — the old boy looked up to me as he swept away the dirt — & said, "Pour la belle Cause, Monsieur." "Oui Monsieur," said I — "suivant vôtre exemple dans tout L'Europe et Vous êtes les imitateurs superbs, — par exemple" — "Monsieur," said he — "Les Francais inventent toujours, et les autres Nations, *perfectionnent!*" — You never saw such a scene, a 12 lb. shot came in at the corner of the roof & went diagonally through the whole House — Doors had been burnt, Wainscots demolished, stalls thrown down, garden walls perforated, flowers crushed, glass broken & every thing not absolutely requisite for shelter destroyed.

I went to seek the but de Chaumont, where the Ecole Polytechnique behaved so well. I could not find it but going into a Cottage hollowed out "Ou est le but de Chaumont?" Up started a little boy about 8 with a red night cap, & with all the air of a Frenchman offered to be my guide. On he marched, and when we came in sight, he turned round like a Grenadier & said, "Monsieur Voila le but de Chaumont" — he then waited for my admiration — & seeing me musing, he turned round as if lost in thought, & said "Quelle belle position! Quelle belle position!" —

I shall go on for ever & tire you out — Fare thee well but not for ever[4] — My Saragossa[5] is gone to the Academy today. I have revised both my Cartoons – & am now going to fly at a Fresco, or Alexander killing a Lion. I do not know which.

My dear Frank has passed his second Examination at Jesus with Eclat & has only one more, & Capt. Phillips has taken my boy Fred with him on board the Howe 120 as the Impregnable is ordered home.

I will send you sketches of their heads – all this does your mind good, as it amuses you.

B. R. Haydon

*Address:* Miss B. Barrett / 50 Wimpole St.
*Postmark:* AP 4 1843

1. "There were at the end of the eighteenth century as many catechisms in use in the French church as there was [*sic*] dioceses . . . ; and since 1785 more than one attempt had been made to standardize them, particularly in the new composite dioceses. To Napoleon this was a heaven-sent opportunity to turn an ecclesiastical reform to political uses. Recourse was had, as in other church matters requiring delicate handling, to Bernier; and his additions to the questions and answers on the fourth commandment, as emended by the Emperor, left no doubt in the minds of his young subjects (if needed they could understand what they were saying) as to what the founder of Christianity really meant when he said, 'Render unto God the things which are God's, and unto Caesar the things which are Caesar's'" (James Matthew Thompson, *Napoleon Bonaparte,* New York, Oxford University Press, 1952, p. 276).

The Imperial Catechism of 1806 does not contain the passage quoted by Haydon, but the sentence seems to paraphrase the following statement concerning the duties of Napoleon's subjects to him: "D[emande]. – N'y a-t-il pas des motifs particuliers qui doivent plus fortement nous attacher à Napoléon premier, notre empereur?

"R[éponse]. – Oui; car il est celui que Dieu a suscité dans les circonstances difficiles, pour rétablir le culte public de la religion sainte de nos pères, et pour en être le protecteur. Il a ramené et conservé l'ordre public, par sa sagesse profonde et active; il défend l'Etat par son bras puissant; il est devenu l'oint du Seigneur, par la consécration qu'il a reçue du souverain pontife, chef de l'Eglise universelle."

(Question. – Are there not special motives which most strongly should attach us to Napoleon I, our emperor? Answer. – Yes; for he is the one whom God has appointed in difficult circumstances to reëstablish the public cult of our father's holy religion, and to be the protector of it. He has led and saved the public order, by his profound and active wisdom; he defends the State by his powerful arm; he has become the anointed of the Lord, by the consecration which he has received from the sovereign pontiff, head of the universal church. André Latreille, *Le catéchisme impérial de 1806,* Paris, 1935, p. 81.)

2. Admiral Count Nikolay Semenovich Mordvinov (1754–1845) married Haydon's maternal aunt, Harriet Cobley.

3. In 1831 Sir Robert Peel purchased Haydon's "Napoleon Musing at St. Helena," the first of twenty-three versions of the subject. Wordsworth's sonnet, "To B. R. Haydon, on Seeing his Picture of Napoleon Buonaparte on the Island of St. Helena," was composed on June 11, 1831, and included in Wordsworth's fourth collective edition of 1832.

4. Byron, "Fare thee well! and if for ever," l. 1.

5. "The Maid of Saragossa," finished in 1842 and won in a raffle by James Webb.

# 36

## To Miss Barrett
## April 5, 1843

You Ingenious little darling invisible

The Duke was not in England, & therefore was not one of the Clique who were insensible to the Je viens comme Themistocle & when Blucher hinted putting Napoleon to Death — who expressed indignation? the Duke — Have you read his Despatches?[1] these are the things — you have read every thing of Napoleon — but you have *not* read every thing of the Duke & ergo — your mind is not so well informed on the one as the other — & Ergo, you cannot be an equally just Judge.

I have been to see Hayter's picture today[2] — Brougham[3] was close to me & he seemed in a great passion for he said the finest thing in it were Burdett's boots![4] — the Prime Figure is the door keeper of the House of Commons, he is more prominent than the Duke whose Portrait is very excellent. Altogether it is a work of great labor — the Principles of Art must never be sacrificed in these sort of Works. I have painted Two — the Quakers & the Whigs[5] — if ever I paint a third, I will compose it as if it was an ancient subject — & when settled as a fine Picture put in the heads. Instead of that, or put them as they sit or as they stand and it becomes a burlesque — a Cauliflower of heads & a bunch of Cravats — The best work of Hayter's, a fair specimen of his natural powers, is Lord

William Russell's trial.[6] I don't like the Man, he is a slave—he married a woman older than himself—ill used her—& his Mistress poisoned herself, a very pretty little affair.

I mean to send you drawings of my children—you have seen the Mama—it is right you should see the offspring—you had better let the servant bring down Wordsworth—& be ready in the Hall—so that the Exchange may be quietly managed—I fear disturbing you too much by these letters, Pictures & Messages. Quiet is everything to you. I am delighted at Mary Mitford's success[7]—indeed—I hope to see my dear Friend safely settled.

My eldest boy Frank has passed his second examination at Jesus & has only one more.

Ever yours dear Madam<br>
B. R. Haydon

*Address:* Miss B. Barrett / 50 Wimpole St.
*Postmark:* AP 6 1843

1. Wellington's *Dispatches* from 1799 to 1818 were edited by Colonel John Gurwood and published in London in twelve volumes between 1834 and 1838.
2. Sir George Hayter's "The Meeting of the First Reformed Parliament," exhibited at the Egyptian Hall.
3. Henry Peter Brougham (1778–1868), Baron Brougham and Vaux, the Lord Chancellor.
4. On April 5, 1843, Haydon wrote: "Brougham came in with me, & as he looked at the Picture he said, 'The most striking thing in it is Burdett's breeches. It is outrageously ridiculous to make the door Keeper of the House the most prominent head in it.' This was spitish but true. It is a work of great labor. His best work is Lord William Russell. I have painted two such works—the Quakers & the Whigs, but if I ever paint a third, I'll compose it as if I was composing an ancient Subject & fit on modern heads on principles of Art, not bend principles of art to modern Vanity" (*Diary,* V,259).
5. Haydon completed "The Anti-Slavery Convention" in 1841 and "The Reform Banquet" in 1834. The first depicted delegates, many of them Quakers, to the international meeting of abolitionists held in London in 1840, and the second portrayed the Whigs' victory banquet following passage of the Reform Bill in 1832.
6. In 1825 Hayter painted "The Trial [for High Treason] of Lord William Russell at the Old Bailey in 1683."
7. See Letter 22, note 1.

# 37

---

April 4th 1843

I thank you most earnestly my dear kind friend for only substituting one kindness for another in the withdrawment of the first Wordsworth. Oh what a surprise to me who was in the midst of a sigh for the loss of my vision, – to look up and see – Helvellyn again, my poet again!!! [2] – Try to fancy the surprise it was! – & how a gladness lay perdu in the surprise! – "and a stupidity" you will add, "in the gladness"! – Because certainly I ought not to be surprised at any kindness of yours – I ought to be a connoisseur in it & you by this time! –

I like the new picture even better, in the general combination, than I did the last; although the head of the poet, probably from being less finished, is inferior as a likeness & expression of the individual intellect. But the general combination – the balancement of the scenic nature and the Humanity – is admirable – very grandly & suggestively preserved; the nature not stooping to the man, nor the man dwarfed before the nature – the wild sky & the serene forehead unabashed & unshrinking in the presence of each other. I like too that eagle in the cloud "mewing his mighty strength" [3] in sympathy with the poet-soul underneath him! – What am I that I should be gazing thus, from my sofa, on eagles, & rocks & clouds? How can we talk of low crowns and crooked swords, when we may talk of eagles & rocks & clouds? – Ah – Mr. Haydon! – you bribe me by them ( – do you?) to give up, bound hand & foot to you, *Napoleon;* that you may smite him with the words of your mouth until there is no more hope? – Well – and if I do – will you promise me to smite besides the fair-lipped cold-hearted Austrian wife – Duchess of Parma – worthy daughter of the double Francis [4] – Marie Louise of France? Poor Josephine! Her sorrow avenged her! –

There are two false wives, within the last century, standing cold upon pedestals of alabaster—one of them being called by their admiring publics, *"Innocence"*—the other—*"Virtue"*—Marie Louise and Lady Byron![5] Oh! I know that Lady Byron is of course "wisest virtuousest discreetest best"—but "all that" just makes her odiousest to *me*. Keep my secret for me; & shelter my discretion better than I do myself—which means—*Don't* by any means, Mr. Haydon, if she should happen to be a very particular friend of yours, go & call upon her instantly, on purpose to tell her that I abhor her.

Why shouldn't I have read the Duke's Despatches? How do you come to imagine that I have not read them? How did you come by your adroit guessing?—For the truth is, I really have *not* read them—I had a presentiment that I *couldn't*. Is it your opinion that I, who have the misfortune of not being Marcus Curtius, as you see,—could read those Despatches? Answer me, & decide my reading for me. I have read Caesar's Commentaries, to be sure; but I found them harder to read than his battles were to fight; & as *dry*—as the Rubicon under the Canicular!—

It is *you* who are ingenious? Be ingenuous besides, & confess to me that the Duke of Wellington, although he magnanimously kept the fifth commandment & abstained from assassinating his great enemy, did (absent or present) *approve* & assent in his soul to the Imprisonment on the rock & all the noble items thereto appertaining.

I congratulate you on the success of your children & wish it all double!—my thanks are a hundred times over! Ever your obliged and sincere

Elizabeth B. Barrett

Wordsworth is Laureate. Are you glad? *I* am very glad indeed.

How is it possible that your kindnesses can do me any harm? I should be in a mortal state indeed if they could.

1. Miss Barrett erroneously dated her letter two days early. It obviously replies to Haydon's of April 5 and refers to Wordsworth's acceptance of the poet-laureateship on April 4, announced in the newspapers of April 5.

2. "The picture of Wordsworth climbing Helvellyn [now in the National Portrait Gallery] was evidently replaced by the [unfinished] picture of the poet seated upon Helvellyn [now in Dove Cottage]" (Shackford, p. 65).

3. Milton, *Areopagitica*. "Methinks I see in my mind a noble and puissant Nation rousing herself like a strong man after sleep, and shaking her invincible locks: Methinks I see her as an Eagle muing her mighty youth, and kindling her undazl'd eyes at the full midday beam" (*The Works of John Milton*, New York, Columbia University Press, 1931, IV,344).

4. Marie Louise, Napoleon's second wife, was the daughter of Archduke Francis, later Emperor Francis I of Austria. After Napoleon's downfall she was known as the Duchess of Parma.

5. "Miss Barrett had been an ardent admirer of Byron's poetic powers. In later years Mrs. Browning heard the other side, from Mrs. Anna Jameson, then a close friend of Lady Byron" (Shackford, p. 66).

# 38

## To Haydon
## April 7, 1843

April 7, 1843,

Oh to be sure my dear Mr. Haydon, *do* send me the letters if you can lay your hand upon them.[1] I wrote a poem once upon Napoleon & published it in the Athenaeum,[2] & if I can lay my hand on *that*, which was written some three years ago, you shall see what I had the insolence to write of *my* hero. Did I call him my hero? — No, no! — he shall not be my hero — except — when you hold up Wellington for yours, right before me, & insist upon my listening to all your excellent good reasons for the same, wrong against me! —

But, Mr. Haydon, — *you* are Marcus Curtius "Juvenis bello egregius"[3] — to say nothing at all of your being Solomon;[4] & therefore it is scarcely fair, I beg you to consider, that I, who am Elizabeth Barrett a woman & unwise, should be exposed to the full fire, drums & trumpets, of your military tactics. And so, if you please, we wont fight like Napoleon & Wellington *about* Napoleon & Wellington, we will leave them to posterity. Certainly you deserve to be opposed to a general of the Empire – you clash your arguments with such iron eloquence. You deserve twice over, to be Curtius – & I tell you so. Moreover, I will tell you something besides. Shall I? Will you be angry? Yes, I will – No, – you wont.

Well, then, this is what I will tell you – i.e. that I am almost satisfied with what your nature has wrung from you on the subject of St. Helena, & St. Helena prisoner too. You admit, perhaps scarcely consciously, but a generous nature would not suffer you to say less – that George the fourth & his generation (inclusive, mark, of your hero) did not comprehend the touch of poetry in Napoleon & his situation – & that to the chivalrous language used by *him,* they answered nothing with their deaf souls. You admit this – and I see clearly through the doubled & tripled pages you have written to me, that you feel the shame of it – that you would rather shut your eyes, than stare upon this stain in our country's escutcheon – that you would give your hopes for your Curtius with posterity, to efface this memory from our Past. – Am I right? Not very wrong, in any case.

Expedient! – to be sure the rock was expedient. May – if they had given him hemlock before he touched it, the expediency would have been undeniable. The ocean-fort dungeon, the friendless desert, the spiritual iron which entered into the soul; much that tortured; all that helped to kill; was very expedient indeed. It was safe – it was prudent – it was nearly wise. Pity that it should also be so ungenerous & so shameful. Pity that it had not magnanimity in *proportion* to the expediency – but this, unhappily it had NOT. Unhappily – for *whom?* Not for Napoleon *now* – but for *us!* – for our dignity among the nations, & our praise with the chronicles of the future.

Oh! that *you* who can prove so much good for Wellington, could prove that he stirred one step, uttered one word, breathed one wish in that great emergency, in order to secure a generous reception of his defenceless foe. Prove that, & Wellington shall be my hero as well as yours – prove that, & he shall be greater to me than ten Waterloos could make him seem to me otherwise. But alas and alas, for him & for England — you cannot prove it.

Possible dangers there might be & were — but an English hero should have remembered that *shame is more dangerous than danger.* The fact pricks me, with regard to this question, like a sword — Alexander of Russia said "If he had come to *me!*"

Your account of your visit to Paris is very interesting — & I should very much like to see your two letters in detail upon the subject.

Napoleon was a great man — Bourrienne a traitor. Bourrienne gave me false impressions before I cross-questioned him with other writers. Napoleon was a great man — with gigantic faults, & certain littlenesses in the grain of the marble. With regard to his kingship, Paul Courier said of him, *"il aspire à descendre,"* & that was the precise verity. Still, he was great — greater than a great conqueror: & if his arms were extended for the seizure of the world, he had a mind large enough to comprehend it. I believe he was sincere in his over-estimate of English generosity in that letter to the Prince Regent. He hated us certainly — but esteem & hatred are compatible — Ask Plutarch else! —

Most truly yours<br>E. B. B.

Our dear friend at Three Mile Cross is prospering in the subscription which has passed the sixteenth hundred: & the debts are *not* understated.

1. See Letter 34, note 8.
2. "Napoleon's Return," *The Athenaeum,* July 4, 1840, p. 532.
3. In *The Annals of the Roman People* (VII,6), Livy thus described Marcus Curtius as "a young soldier of great prowess." A chasm once appeared in the Forum, which could not be filled with earth. Soothsayers declared that the chief strength of the Roman people must be offered as a sacrifice. Believing that the gods thus demanded the death of a soldier, as a patriotic duty Curtius rode his horse into the chasm, from which, of course, they never emerged. Haydon melodramatically depicted this plunge in six pictures entitled "Curtius Leaping into the Gulf," painted in 1842, 1843, and 1844, with his own face resembling that of Curtius.

4. Solomon, in Haydon's "The Judgment of Solomon," finished in 1814, seems to be an idealized self-portrait of the artist. Haydon informed Miss Barrett that he was the model for Curtius and Solomon in Letter 28.

# 39

## To Miss Barrett
## April 8, 1843

London April 8th 1843

My dearest Friend,

Read his Despatches bit by bit, Volume by Volume, line by line, every one – they are as fine as any thing in the World, finer than the Commentaries, a million times, & prove him to be a greater Man than Caesar; they are applicable to all humanity – they will & must be recommended to youth of all professions, they are as generally & morally beautiful as any Young Man's Companion. They are as generally applicable as Reynolds' lectures, and there is not the slightest taint of bombast, imposture, or falsehood like the trash of Napoleon's bulletins – Read them, My dearest Friend, but read them with *Faith* – Get interested, as you do, in Richardson's Novels – Wade [through] the Volume 1st – you are not military, but the 1st Vol. is so – but still read it as a duty.

There is a letter in the Despatches to Colville[1] (I think) softening his disappointment at not being made a Peer, *exquisite* – Read that, I think I am right as to name. "If anything could have compensated me" (said I think Colville) "for not getting my reward, it was the Duke's letter" – & *well he might say so.*

The fact is, you invisible Napoleonette, you do not know the Duke – His perfect Completeness of Character. But you do know *Lady Byron.* I'll send you one of my lectures on Fuzeli, in which I allude to that double X icicle, Lady B.[2] I only came in contact twice with her[3] – & we quarrelled without hope, the second time – the first day, I thought Byron a brute – the second day I was convinced *she* was – a Mathematician.

> The morning dress was dimity,
> The Evening silk.[4]

Think of the Cant of Women & Men. She refused him once because it was *proper* to be *sought* – By Heaven I should have liked to have seen the Woman who would have refused me in the flush of Youth – *because it was proper!* She should have had all the propriety to herself – I have a theory – perhaps you will be very angry – it is this – A Man who is ever refused must be an XXX – because no Man would ever propose, who was not first quite sure of being agreable. Miranda is my Woman. Mary is Miranda – She did not run away when I had an execution – her Friends said it was not proper to follow me to Prison[5] – but go to her Mother's – they were to come next day – and directly they were gone in solemn humbug she took a Coach & drove down to me – Frank was then a Baby – that's my Woman & that was Byron's – but the refusal of Miss Chaworth destroyed his mind –

I heard from Wordsworth today[6] – he sent Mary some touching lines on Grace Darling, which I enclose, and which you must return, or Lord have mercy on us both. I regret he was prevailed on to be *honorary* laureate for that he tells me is the condition – in his 74th Year, with his foes prostrate & his Genius acknowledged, he should have gone out of the World on his own Pinions alone!!! This is the way great principles are compromised, that Men may escape the imputation of not being polite. I was on the point of writing him a letter saying "I am delighted you did not accept the laureatship – if you had, you old Lake Poet – I would have taken out all your sonnets & danced upon them!" Now what shall I do? – there is one thing sure – I shall have no more this I fear is his weak point – Keats & I years ago – could tell you something but you will read my Memoirs when I am gone.[7] O God grant me One Year before I die, of clear, powerful, lucid, intellectual power, unencumbered, to give the World my records of 40 years.

Adieu – Napoleonettina

B. R. Haydon

*Address:* Miss B. Barrett / 50 Wimpole St.
*Postmark:* AP 10 1843

1. Sir Charles Colville (1770–1843), who served with distinction in the Peninsular War.
2. In lecturing on Fuseli on June 14, 1839, Haydon spoke of the shock to a man of genius on being recalled from concentration by trivialities of everyday life. Byron, persecuted by spies and alienists engaged by Lady Byron, is used as an example (*Lectures*, II,22).
3. Lady Byron sat to Haydon on July 2 and 3, 1840, for her portrait in "The Anti-Slavery Convention."
4. Byron, *Don Juan*, I,xii,94–95. "Her morning dress was dimity, / Her evening silk!"
5. Haydon referred to the first of his four imprisonments for debt, from May 22 to July 26, 1823.
6. The letter was written on April 6, 1843 (*The Letters of William and Dorothy Wordsworth*, ed. Ernest De Selincourt, Oxford, Oxford University Press, 1939, III,1160–1161).
7. Haydon probably referred to the letter dated March 21, 1818, in which Keats wrote to him: "It is a great Pity that People should by associating themselves with the finest things, spoil them ... Wordsworth has damned the lakes" (*The Letters of John Keats*, ed. Hyder Edward Rollins, Cambridge, Mass., Harvard University Press, 1958, I,251–252).

# *40*

---

## *To Miss Barrett*
## *April 8, 1843*

London Sat Night Apr 8 1843

That was not kind of me to say that of dear Wordsworth – burn the letter – I beg – he seems melancholy, at burying Southey,[1] and talks of his best days being over. I enclose you his letter which pray return with Grace Darling. I have been all day going through the whole of preparing & running lime like the thorough bred old Masters—How Artists can call any thing *troublesome* in my glorious Art I know not—I say as Napoleon said, "Je ne connais pas le mot—*Impossible*"; so say I of trouble & impatience in Art; I love all [that] belongs to it & have done so from 8 years old—I built up in my Father's Attic a room of pasteboard, with a Window—here I used to hurry home from School to my darling solitude & Etch—& Sketch—& muse. When I kept a Man Servant—I used to envy the rascal cleaning my brushes! I have two Tons of Lime 25 miles from Town under ground—going through the process of being mellowed—the Lime I fitted today is old—& has been 1 year & 8 months in my cellar—I have made today the regular Bianco St. Giovanni of Cennini—you mix fine lime slaked for a year with water, run it through a sieve, let it settle, throw off the Water, squeeze the rest in a cloth, and the residue let dry [until] it is like butter, it is for this design over my Chimney Piece [*a sketch*].

You have no idea how very wretched I feel without a great work, I want that between me & adversity—I feel protected before a great Canvas or Wall—experience extasies at the excitement of an Intonaco—& glory in brushes, oil, lime, & Imagination!—The Virgin & Child—Each side will be two Arch Angels—Uriel & Michael—I'll tickle ye for a Michael![2]

I got through my Cartoons March 15; ever since that I have been revising & fiddle faddling.

I entered Paris 1814 the very day Josephine died![3] "Ah Monsieur," said a little active Garcon, "Josephine est morte!! Sa christi, ah Monsieur—Pas de Fortune pour Napoleon après Divorce—C'est Vrai." "Avez vous été Soldat?" said I—"Oui Monsieur"—"Ou?"—"à la bataille de Rivoli"—"Ah"—"Oui!" —Wilkie said to me, "Haydon, give me a Glass"—"oui Monsieur," said the Waiter, & he brought him a *Glace* to Wilkie's infinite wonder—Wilkie carried a pocket Dictionary & used to look out the Words—"Garcon"—he used to roar out—"Oui Monsieur"—"donnez moi"—then he'd look out (while I was dying) a spoon—"Une cuillere!!" Wilkie used to say—"don't tell me Haydon"—though Paris was full of all the Nations on Earth—the greatest curiosity was David Wilkie! his long battling with Madame who sat enthroned at the Restaurateur's—about change—was exquisite!—There he would stay till every sous was correct—battling with her in bad French —she, with all the grace of a French Woman putting her pretty fingers on his impenetrable arm, as impenetrable as Auld Reekie hersel! "Mais, Monsieur," "No, no—Madam"— 10 minutes have elapsed & he always got the day & then joined me, chuckling at having made her give up his fair change![4] We had a great deal of fun, I soon knocked him up; he would not go to Rambouillet—I started before he was up and when I came back I found him looking out for me in the Streets of Versailles—with an air of Despair like a man alone in the desert of Zaara. Poor Dear Wilkie—the simplicity of his mind was exquisite—his understanding acute but slow—he had beautiful powers of observation—but he never made impression on Woman's heart—& thus broke his at last, for that is the *real truth*—he left England from sheer restlessness & misery of mind, to wear away reflection; how remarkable I wrote his Sister a letter, saying if he go to Syria he will never return.[5] She replied he could not suffer more than he had done in Ireland—but I said remember the Climate —Poor fellow, I never saw him after—

B. R. Haydon

*Address:* Miss B. Barrett / 50 Wimpole St.
*Postmark:* AP 10 1843

1. Robert Southey died on March 21, 1843.
2. *Henry IV, Part 1,* II,iv,489. "Nay, I'll tickle ye for a young prince, i' faith."
3. Empress Josephine died at Malmaison on May 24, 1814. Wilkie's diary shows that he and Haydon reached Paris on May 31 (Allan Cunningham, *The Life of Sir David Wilkie,* London, John Murray, 1843, I,394).
4. "Notwithstanding Paris was filled with all the nations of the earth, the greatest oddity in it was unquestionably David Wilkie. His horrible French, his strange, tottering, feeble, pale look, his carrying about his prints to make bargains with printsellers, his resolute determination never to leave the restaurants till he got all his change right to a centime; his long disputes about *sous* and *demisous* with the *dame du comptoir;* whilst

madame tried to cheat him, and as she pressed her pretty ringed fingers on his arm without making the least impression, her '*Mais, Monsieur,*' and his Scotch '*Mais, Madame,*' were worthy of Molière" (*Autobiography,* I,194–195).

5. After eight months of travel in Germany, Austria, Turkey, Syria, Palestine, and Egypt, Wilkie died at sea on his homeward voyage on June 1, 1841.

# 41

## *To Miss Barrett*
## *April 18–19, 1843*

London April 18 1843

When a woman says I wont – she is getting better – I foresee health & spirits in your *I wont* be called Napoleonette – all I can reply is that you shall not – and if your dignity be offended, I make the requisite & necessary apology. I saw Mrs. S. C. Hall[1] who is a delightful woman yesterday week, & *we both* agreed about your Poetry; she said she understood every word, & I said the same and we both held forth on your Genius – wont that put you in a superb humour? – did I not say pas Fortune instead of Point de Fortune[2] – you will find in the course of Time, that my French, Italian, Greek, Latin, & Spanish is pretty much on a par. I have no organ of language, & never get on except by association or hearing one spoken – In consequence of Wilkie's life,[3] I have taken up my own, his letters to me are infinitely more natural than his slavish trash to the great – "It's a *grate* thing," said Wilkie, "to be acquainted with the *grate* on pleasant terms – but it is a *grate* thing to know them on *any* terms!!!" Ah Wilkie. Murray wont give me the Book & I am too poor to buy it, I wish you could at your Library borrow it & lend it to me – is it possible?

My dearest Friend? – I have added 10 more pages to my life, and 2 letters of his – I shall go on arranging every thing from my journals under each year – in going through a Journal if there be nothing to conceal – I shall send one down for you to have an idea of what it is full of Sketches & thoughts – Who do you think would treat for my life & correspondence, would Bentley[4] – I do not want to leave it to be done by others – after such omissions & ignorances as Wilkie's displays – Good Night –

April 19 – 1843

I have just got Alexander the Great's head in – killing a Lion. It will be a fine contrast, the Lion with something of Alexander, & Alexander with more of the Lion, fierce – handsome – flushed – conscious of Victory – his Eyes burning, as he catches the glare of the Royal Animal. After great anxiety which to take to, as both are forlorn hopes, as to *sale* – I thought I had better go through Alexander & go on with the Fresco over my chimney when I could be certain of a Month's quiet – which cannot be commanded now. My ammunition is all ready – but the longer it remains the less danger – though my Angel in Fresco, done at once without care of time – has stood & will stand now as long as the Wall – You must know I have an immortal Urn which has made tea for so many immortals – I have had their names let in in a silver plate – now I hope it will last another 25 years – & therefore I am resolved to have your name on the other plate when that is let in – so if you will let me send the Urn down that you may make tea or have it made, from the Immortal – I will send for it again – & so will begin for the other batch with B. Barrett. I'll send Iron & all – and it must go through the regular progress of heating, boiling, & making tea as if you drank tea with me – Is it not a beautiful bit of original thinking – When Geniuses like you & I begin to correspond there will be no end to our inventions! – If the paper scents of color don't be shocked. I must go to work again so good bye till the evening.

9 o'clock

My dear & oldest Friend William Hamilton (Aegyptiaca Hamilton)[5] called & thinks the head of Alexander excellent – I believe *he is right.* I finished my Cartoon 15 of March, I then revised both which occupied a fortnight, I did trifles necessary,

but I had nothing to concentrate my mind on & it fretted —
today I flew at Alexander & have been happy all day. Does the
Athenaeum contain any remarks on Wilkie's life? [6] — if so —
will you lend it? In my correspondence he unravelled himself
& there you see the man — in his correspondence with the
great you did not see the Man he was acting.

He was always acting after the blow the Academy gave him
1830 [7] — & he died worth 30,000 in consequence. I have never
been acting & shall die in a Whig Union. [8]

Are you writing anything? — you surely must be — do tell
me — & what?

You defend Wordsworth gloriously but I regret it, not your
defence but his acceptance.

Good night my dearest Friend

Ever yours

B. R. Haydon

Mary begs her respects. Will you get the Miniatures carefully ready? She is flattered you are pleased.

*Address:* Miss B. Barrett / 50 Wimpole St.
*Postmark:* AP 20 1843

---

1. Mrs. Samuel Carter Hall (Anna Maria Hall, 1800–1881), novelist and
miscellaneous writer.

2. In Haydon's second letter of April 8 to Miss Barrett (Letter 40), he wrote,
"Pas de Fortune pour Napoleon après Divorce."

3. Allan Cunningham's three-volume *Life of Sir David Wilkie* had just
been published by John Murray.

4. Richard Bentley (1794–1871), publisher.

5. William Richard Hamilton (1777–1859), antiquary, diplomatist, and
author of *Aegyptiaca* (London, 1809), containing the first translations of
the inscriptions on the Rosetta Stone, which Hamilton had secured for Great
Britain.

6. Cunningham's *Wilkie* received the leading review in *The Athenaeum*
of April 15, 1843 (pp. 357–359). The review was continued in the issues of
April 22 (pp. 386–389) and April 29 (pp. 411–412).

7. On January 25, 1830, following the death of Sir Thomas Lawrence,
Martin Archer Shee was elected president of the Royal Academy. Wilkie had
expected the honor.

8. A poorhouse or workhouse.

# 42

## To Haydon
## April 21, 1843

April, 1843
Friday

Nothing is impossible said Napoleon—certainly not that I should procure for you the reading of Sir David Wilkie's Life —& you shall have it accordingly, together with the Athenaeum & Examiner critiques upon it.[1] The extracts given in the latter affect one painfully through the inferiority of what Victor Cousin distinguishes as *"l'homme"* from "le grand homme"? The writer of certain subservient letters not only *"acted,"* but acted low comedy parts. Better to die in the "whig union," than to live on opulently, with one's soul & its nobility coined into thirty thousand sovereigns!—Better & happier & more worthy, to die *so!* and yet I hope you never may die so! I hope you wrote those words, my dear Mr. Haydon, rather in self approbation than in despondency; rather in assent to the moral superiority of the "whig union" position, than in anticipation & personal application of its evils. You are yet in the middle of your career & should not wonder at the dust of your own chariot. The goal will bring repose & a clearer air.

In the meantime the Wilkie biography has excited you back again into your own—& I am very glad indeed of it. Oh-do-do-send me the ms.—the journal—anything you dare trust with me: & remember that albeit a woman I can keep a secret pretty well. As to the *publication,* there will be no difficulty about it—only do not part with the ms. with too much facility. Bentley would be glad, I should think, to purchase it; as would Saunders & Otley, Colburn—Whittaker perhaps. I am not personally acquainted with any of these booksellers—& they look so coldly on the genus *poet,* that I doubt whether my own publisher Saunders would stretch out his hand to you with the least degree more courtesy from any introduction I could give you. Nevertheless your work appears to me of a very saleable character: *you should have money for it.* One previous consideration is that you could scarcely name the names of living persons & discuss their merits quite as frankly & freely now, as if the publication were to take place hereafter. If you publish now, you must soften a little – & I would moreover, if I were you, abbreviate & subdue certain parts of your ms. – particularly the opening of it where you speak boldly & openly of your own genius. I like the consciousness of genius, & I do not object to truth under any aspect. But you must be aware that the world & the great mass of readers are irritated by assertion into denial; & are apt to call all such gloryings, if not mistaken sanity, mispoken bad taste. I would therefore if I were you, *spare the provocative.* Now remember – this is not to advise insincerity, but simply one shade more of *reserve* – ! and really it just strikes me that you have every reason for returning my counsel back to me, & that I am growing impertinent. Forgive the impertinence – the freedom! – When the lion roars, he need not say "I am a lion": we know it while we stand beside the wood. And the conventional tactics & proprieties of this age are such, that if he *should* say "I am a lion," all the monkeys on the palm trees are sworn to cry out – "*No* lion! but a jackall."

The urn, the urn! – And you and Mrs. S. C. Hall! – Is it possible? Two people in the world understand "every word" of me! – ! – I ought indeed to be in "a superb humour." I oughtn't indeed to say "I wont" again, altho' I were to grow ever so much better & stronger: No acme of convalescence could justify it! – I am to drink tea with the Immortals! – And two intelligent persons can understand what I say! Why, indeed, dear Mr. Haydon, I grow giddy with prosperity.

But seriously – for we all come to seriousness at last, & *I* sooner than most people – I am grateful to both of you for understanding me, & for having a good hope of my futurity. All my earthly futurity as an individual, lies in poetry. In other respects, the game is up.[2] If it were not for this poetry which I feel within as a destiny to be worked out, I think I should wish to die tomorrow – that is, as far as relates to my own will, & apart from the pain my dying would give to the few immediately connected with me. But poetry which came first, lingers last, it is like a *will to be written*. How I understand you, with your Alexander thrust in defence between you & the actual! – May the thorns not pierce through! –

Mrs. S. C. Hall is an agreeable & graceful writer, & I am one of her many readers, & am glad to be able to put by her name among those who are my friends through kindness. From her husband I had one or two kind notes once, when he had the editorship of Colburn's Magazine,[3] & I was a contributor to the same.

But the urn, the urn – what am I to say? You do me too much honor Mr. Haydon – *that* is the first thing to say. And being unworthy, should I accept it? Ah – perhaps no! Well – if you send it – (but reconsider the matter & do not send, if you have misgivings) – if you send it, I will look at it reverently & try to be worthier from this time forwards. Or shall I propose a compromise; & instead of drinking tea from it, drink hot water in abasement of spirit? Peradventure *that* would be "the more excellent way."

I like your Alexander with the lion's look in him, & your lion with Alexander's! – It is true of you, what I have repeatedly heard admitted by those who are coldest in your praise; that "Haydon is certainly a poetical painter." You are very poetical in your conceptions – may your Alexander conquer a new world for you!

As for languages, there is no lower attainment! – If I ever worked hard at Greek, it was for poetry's sake purely.

Ever sincerely yours<br>E. B. B.

Our friend, dear Miss Mitford, sets out next Tuesday for Devonshire, & intends to be some three weeks or a month away.

May I offer my thankful acknowledgments to Mrs. Haydon

for her kind message? I hope I may have the pleasure one day of making her personal acquaintance, notwithstanding that terrible oath taken by one of us!—the miniatures shall be ready.

Here are the Examiner & Athenaeum, which you may keep. I have sent to the library for Wilkie's Life, & am promised it "in a few days." I suppose the first reading has been seized upon.

1. As Professor Shackford pointed out (p. 69), these reviews appeared in both publications for April 15. This fact led her to date the letter "April, Friday [21?], 1843"; it is obviously an answer to Haydon's letter of April 18.
2. *Cymbeline*, III,iii,107.
3. Samuel Carter Hall (1800–1889) edited Henry Colburn's *New Monthly Magazine* from 1832 to 1836.

# 43

## *To Miss Barrett*
## *April 22, 1843*

London Apr 22 1843

My dearest Friend,

I send you the Urn, out of which Apollo would be proud to drink tea with the Nine!—and I promise thee if thou canst on thy sacred poetical word assure me thou hast bona fide had the Servant to heat the *very* Iron, put the boiling water into the *very* Urn—& made your *tea* from the *very* Urn & drank *it* legitimately—& no mistake that thy poetical name shall be the first on the very next inscription—on the other side.

I have been to see a dear old Friend today, Smirke [1]—more than 90 years old—he who encouraged me when Northcote depressed me 39 years ago—He was delighted & has promised to come & see the Cartoons—He said I had the same face as at 18 but my head was bald & my hair grey.

I have finished up to 1810 the end of my Memoirs & will send you some journals in a day or two, wherein there is nothing which might offend your Mind.

Adieu—I have been all day out flying about—I think I have sold Curtius as a Draper sells broad cloth—"What is the price?" "5.5. Sir."—"I'll give £2.10—& no more"—"you shan't have it."—"I won't go beyond £3.10." "Well, Sir, I suppose I must take it"—Oh this beastly commercial spirit!

B. R. Haydon

*Address:* Miss B. Barrett / 50 Wimpole St.

1. Robert Smirke (1752–1845), R.A., genre painter and book illustrator.
2. See Letter 12, note 3.

# 44

## *To Miss Barrett*
## *April 25, 1843*

London April 25 1843

My dearest Friend,

Your advice is excellent but I think my reasons for not taking it are good too.

If Men who are acknowledged to be Men of Genius were permitted to detail their early & progressive feelings without concealment there would not be such doubt about the faculty; I know the leading passion of human nature is hatred of superiority, and I know that any Man who has the Art like Wilkie to believe himself nothing, or affect it, is much more quietly born testimony to, than one who believes himself gifted & does not conceal it. Be assured Wellington believed it of himself, but Wellington did not like Napoleon avow it. Wellington is therefore the more perfect character of the two, but I like notwithstanding the "voyez cet êtoile" of Napoleon—It is a matter of Character.

Confidentially I ask you, what made me write? I don't know now a single rule of Composition—I got in a passion with Sir George—people said who wrote that for you?—I said nobody—it is very well written was the reply—I reflected if this is to write well I can always do it—when I am in a passion.

Wilkie said your conception of Dentatus [1] is very fine. Why? —your lines are repeated—your groups are divided & yet United—& from what he said of my composition, I laid down rules to compose—though I had actually composed it without being acquainted with a single rule! I say to detail all the feelings of such a mind, don't laugh (great or small) from beginning to feel will be useful to the Student & the World— The pleasure I feel in writing you is because you let me talk so much of myself. I really declare to you I am not conceited because I leave nothing undone—but I was so much astonished at being called a Man of Genius that I began to investigate the nature of the faculty which had produced what the World called so, and this is the real motive—I never paint a hand without drawing it first—or a Picture without making a sketch—I paint every thing from nature down to a spear handle—Is this conceit?

Therefore I will hazard a Rousseau sort of confession of feeling—from childhood to manhood—and on. Wilkie & I were so extremely intimate till—till—I must not tell you at *present* —or you will say, was there ever such an invincible puppy?— and his correspondence wherein the *real* Man is seen, will form part when I have got 300 pages ready—I will take your advice—I am now at the 220th.

I shall take up & do justice to the Hunts,[2] men who have had such an effect on their connections for Evil & for good— John Hunt was the noblest specimen of a human being I ever met. His affection for a Friend rose to blood heat, as his Friend sunk to adversity; Wilkie's always sunk below Zero, exactly as misfortune depressed his Friend—Leigh was equally affectionate, but so insufferably selfish from incarnate Vanity that his heart was stifled by self Love; & poor Robert, obscure & unknown, had the warmth of both without the ability. I met him once in the street when I was painting Solomon—"how are you," said he—"dreadfully anxious"—"Why?"—"I have got 58 to pay today & have only got 50, I am going to try if that will do for a week"—"My dear Haydon stop a moment"—he darted off round a corner, & in 10 minutes brought me £8, squeezed my hand & said—"Let me have it as soon as possible"—What do you think he did—raised it on his watch! that's the history of the whole *three*—Do you think such hearts don't take the lead in the Deity's eyes! Oh Yes—

From your station, perhaps, you will not enter into this—as I do—perhaps you may be shocked at a Man raising money on his Watch to help his Friend—This was the bond between us all till Leigh Hunt's despotism of Conceit became insufferable—Every body he touched he soiled, Byron, Moore, Wordsworth, Wilkie & myself—and all were obliged to let him go—Keats too—was obliged.

John Keats was a noble natural Gentleman—no polish—no education—but well bred, from dignity of right feeling I never respected any Man so much—

Albert has commissioned Eastlake, M'Clise & Ross to fresco a Summer House in Buckingham Palace.

I hope you enjoyed the Urn—

Goodnight

B. R. Haydon

*Address:* Miss B. Barrett / 50 Wimpole St.
*Postmark:* AP 26 1843

1. Haydon's second picture, "The Assassination of Dentatus," painted for Lord Mulgrave in 1808 and 1809.
2. The Hunt brothers—John (1775–1848), Leigh (1784–1859), and Robert (c.1773–1850)—associates in publishing the *Examiner* from 1808 to 1825. John and Leigh were imprisoned from 1813 to 1815 for libeling the Prince Regent. Robert reviewed art exhibits.

# 45

---

*To Miss Barrett*
*April 28, 1843*

London April 28 1843

My Dearest Friend

I send you two Sketches of Napoleon's favorite little column at the end of his Jardin Anglais & his bed, which was magnificent—Green Lyons Velvet with painted Roses on white satin—four Greek casques with Ostrich plumes at the top, & a border of gold lace a yard white [wide]—Finish a looking glass—

Will you return the immortal Urn.

I have been sadly shocked at reading Wilkie's life—to think that for 20 years of our earliest Friendship when daily I used to read to him my journal of my thoughts—& he used to speak of the danger of all personal remarks in a journal, which I never did. It was only a journal of conclusions on Art & Poetry which have been the foundation of my Lectures—I am shocked that I never knew *he* kept a journal of nothing but remarks on his Friends, their weaknesses & follies. He must, like a Fox, have gone to his bed room night after night —& wrote down his journal. In all our journies I never saw a symptom—& never knew he had one. I do not know I was ever more pained because it shewed the value of his heart, or rather *Scotch* pebble.

Is it not shocking? I shall be obliged to say something.

Yours ever & ever

B. R. Haydon

I'll exchange the sketches in a week.

*Address:* Miss B. Barrett / 50 Wimpole St.

# 46

*To Haydon*
*April 29, 1843*

April 29, 1843.

This is my certificate, my dear Mr. Haydon, that I have taken & Quaffed a cup of emreeta[1] from your urn of the Immortals! And seeing that my dog Flush did take & quaff of the lees of my cup, this is also a humble suggestion that in the case of your carrying into practice your talk of honoring me in a second inscription, you do inscribe the worthy name of Flush first & my name afterwards—we two completing together a very perfect antithesis to your *Dii Majores.*

For the rest, the urn was going to you when you sent, & I am sensible that I ought not to have kept it so long. Thank you for the memorials of Fontainbleau—thank you twenty times. So it was under Lyons velvet that he passed the agony of his kingship? it was yard-wide gold lace which throbbed to the throbbing of his great heart? Poor Napoleon!

You amused me by your flattering naiveté of liking to write to me *because* I let you write of yourself!—Well! I may always promise you such a reason for liking to write to me—and I do.

When you differ from me, understand distinctly that I never advocated *hypocrisy.* An assumed humility is the most odious of the forms of vanity and Truth under every form is noble. What I said a word in favor of, was no hypocrisy—but reserve —just what Carlyle describes excellently in his new work, —"Leave it to your enemies to praise you—or at least to your friends,"[2] Nevertheless you may be right in your particular case—I will not say that you are not: and I quite believe for my own part, that no high power exists without the possessor being conscious of it; that, according to my figure, the lion knows always that he can roar.

I am anxious, you see, for the success of the Biography— judge whether I must not be, for its progress. Your manner

April 29. 1843.

This is my certificate my dear Mr. Haydon, that I have taken & quaffed a cup of enthusiasm from your urn of the Immortals! And seeing that my dog Flush did take & quaff of the lees of my cup, there is also a humble suggestion that in the case of your carrying into practice your talk of honoring me in a second inscription, you do inscribe the worthy name of Flush first & my name afterwards .. we two completing together a very perfect antithesis to your Dii majores.

As to the rest, the urn was going to you when you sent, & I am sensible that I ought not to have left it so long. Thank you for the memorials of Sotaintheaw —

of writing, if not always correct & classical, is always characteristic & vivacious – & Wilkie's is pale & common by the side of it – which remark I make only from the extracts in reviews & not from the book itself as I have not seen it. To two separate booksellers, have I sent for this book – & they answer, *"in a few days"* – which vexes me because I wanted it for you. Tell me – have you seen it? I suspect that you have seen it & read it, by what you say; & because, in the extracts I sent you in the reviews, there was surely nothing offensive to you. It appears that he has spoken [3]

1. The *Oxford English Dictionary* lists this Sanscrit-derived word (also spelled *amrita*) as an adjective meaning "immortal, ambrosial," introduced into English in 1810 by Robert Southey in *The Curse of Kehama.*
2. Thomas Carlyle, *Past and Present*, London, Chapman and Hall, 1843.
3. The letter is incomplete, as the second sheet has been lost. Although dated, perhaps erroneously, the day before Haydon wrote Letter 47, he had not received it at that time.

# 47

*To Miss Barrett*
*April 30, 1843*

Sunday Apr. 30 1843

My dearest Madam,

I am afraid you are ill! – not a line even on the Urn!

I am now come to Leigh Hunt in my life – and as soon as I get to page 300 – I shall send it to you – Was not that I told you of one of the Brothers, a touching fact of a good heart – indeed I assure you John Hunt principally aided me at that time through the Picture of Solomon – the folly of Leigh has broken up the whole family –

Have you got Wilkie's life – I have read the first & the 3rd, the 2nd I have not seen. Your admirable remarks on his character are capital – I have to tell my story yet – & tell it

I will—It is lamentable to me a mind so enslaved as his mind was & a disposition being kicked in proportion to submission. All his letters to his Patrons are pieces of the grossest acting—Cunningham left out the latter part of one of his letters feeling it to be so degrading—luckily I had a *copy*, or I should not have known it!—Is it not shocking? I assure you my indignation at his abominable usage by the Academy was the principal instigation, more than my own wrongs, to attack the vices of that body—and directly after *he* refused to be seen with me in the Streets![1]

If you like I will send you my Evidence before the Committee of the House.[2]

I am hard at work on Alexander but my dear Daughter's danger harrasses my mind—I do not think she will recover.

I am My dear Friend

Ever yours

B. R. Haydon

*Address:* Miss B. Barrett / 50 Wimpole St.

1. Haydon probably referred to events in 1810, when Wilkie sent "The Man with the Girl's Cap" to the Royal Academy's exhibition but withdrew it because the Council considered Edward Bird's "The Game of Put" and "Village Choristers" superior pictures of the same type (Allan Cunningham, *The Life of Sir David Wilkie*, 3 vols., London, 1843, I,289). Although Haydon did not publicly champion Wilkie in this matter, he strongly attacked the Royal Academy in letters appearing in the *Examiner* in 1812. On December 22, 1836, Haydon wrote: "[Wilkie] seemed much annoyed at my saying in my evidence that he had been frightened at being seen with me in the Streets after my attack on the Academy. I told him it was *true*, which he did not deny, because it was. We had breakfasted with Seguier after the attack, & on coming out he said, 'It would not be right to be seen *with you*,' & went away" (*Diary*, IV,392).

2. On June 28, 1836, Haydon gave evidence before the Select Committee on Arts and Principles of Design.

# 48

*To Miss Barrett*
*May 4, 1843*

London May 4th 1843

My dearest Friend,

I am bitterly touched to tell you — a *decline* exists, which I have long suspected — & today it has been confirmed by medical report![1] — Mary has not been told and what to do I do not know, pretty dear she has had an anxious life, & will perhaps be glad to escape —

I fear she was not nourished by Society at a budding time — when most girls acquire admiration — & lovers —

God knows, I shall do nothing but reflect on myself.

Yours affectionately,

B. R. Haydon

Tell Mary Mitford if you write her. I am happy you have changed rooms[2] — take *care* — *take* care. God bless you, my sweetest Friend.

*Address:* Miss B. Barrett / 50 Wimpole St.
*Postmark:* MY 4 1843

1. Entries in his diary for this period show Haydon's anxiety about his daughter's health. Later letters to Miss Barrett discuss this.

2. One may infer that Miss Barrett's lost letter to which this replies contained a reference to her cloistered existence at 50 Wimpole Street similar to her remarks to Miss Mitford, to whom, on May 4, 1843, she wrote: "I have come into Papa's room, the adjoining room to mine, — for the first time today — to have the windows opened and a little dusting done — which will make me cleaner and more exemplary tomorrow. The consequence of living through the winter in one room, with a fire, day and night, and every crevice sealed close, — you may imagine perhaps by the help of your ideal of all Dustlessness, latent and developped" (Miller, p. 178).

# 49

*To Miss Barrett*
*May 6, 1843*

London May 6th 1843

My sweetest Friend,

Your letter has done more good, than bottles of physic – I trust in God, she will weather it, the dear Girl. I reproach myself for my too great pressure on all their *budding* Intellects – making no allowance for their age – She never spits – blood or any thing else – she has no pain in her side – but she wastes – has no relish for food or existence! I trust in God – She is my only daughter[1] – & was a splendid Girl – as fine a figure as ever moved! Mary is dreadfully affected – your letter has delighted them both – I think if you would write 20 lines to Mrs. Haydon yourself it would be a great balm – and my *daughter* too – It would please them.

Are you inclined to see a Comic Picture of Mine in the midst of Alexander, "The first child *very* like *about* the eyes, & not so like *about the nose.*"[2] These are the darts sorrow shoots out of the mind,[3] Antony says.

I sat yesterday to a Man[4] who kept me 2 hours & half without painting a touch – measuring, sticking compasses into nose, chin, & forehead and thinks himself a Genius.

I am delighted you are not worse for your first move. Your living is a miracle which ought to support the dying.

God bless you<br>B. R. Haydon

*Address:* Miss B. Barrett / 50 Wimpole St.
*Postmark:* MY 6 1843

1. By this time five of Haydon's children, including two daughters, had died in infancy.
2. Haydon painted the first version of this picture in 1831. He began his second version on May 4, 1843.
3. *Antony and Cleopatra*, IV,ii,14–15. " 'Tis one of those odd tricks which sorrow shoots / Out of the mind."

4. Haydon's diary for May 6, 1843, contains two allusions to this portrait painter, but unfortunately they have both been heavily scratched out. The latest known portrait of Haydon was painted by Thomas Henry Illidge in 1838, and is used as a frontispiece to this book.

# 50

*To Miss Barrett*
*May 9, 1843*

London May 9 1843

My dear Miss Barrett,

You are quite right—my eagerness would lead you astray—in feminine Etiquette—The Exhibition is open,[1] my Saragossa is there, but it is too high to see the Execution or expressions—M'Clise is a clever fellow but hideous taste—Costume run Mad—Stone has a touching thing the last appeal—a young pale agitated lover, appealing once more to a sweet girl who is pained at still saying *"it's useless."* I felt for the poor fellow—an absolute pang—poor fellow, his face is the picture of that mysterious agony! and yet she is not a coquette, but a fine feeling creature who *can't* love him—confound that Stone—a very nice fellow but an absolute executioner—

I have done 100 pages of Memoir & have touched up Leigh Hunt & got through our Controversy about Negro faculties[2] 1811 in which I fleshed my maiden pen!

Adieu—I shall exchange Sketches.

My daughter is really not so weak—I hope for the best. Mrs. Haydon & she beg kindest regards—

Ever yours
B. R. Haydon

The Duke has bought my old Friend Sir W. Allan's Waterloo.

*Address:* Miss B. Barrett / 50 Wimpole St.
*Postmark:* MY 10 1843

1. At the Royal Academy's exhibition, which opened on May 8, 1843, Haydon exhibited "The Maid of Saragossa."

2. Haydon's four letters contending that blacks were inferior to whites were published in the *Examiner* of September 1 (p. 566), September 15 (p. 596), September 22 (p. 611), and September 29, 1811 (p. 629). They were signed with his pseudonym, "An English Student."

# 51

## *To Miss Barrett*
## *May 11, 1843*

London May 11 1843

My dearest Friend,

Saragossa is at the Academy, nearer Heaven than it ever was before, or ever will be again. It is painful to see such malignity—the very Men Shee, Phillips, & Howard, who 34 years ago used Dentatus so shamefully[1] had influence again this year and though I saw them all before a Committee[2] & saw them pale & standing like Culprits as a bit of moral justice, they could not in their hearts let such an opportunity escape of giving another Mumbling bite with their withered toothless gums before they drop into the grave which yawns to receive them putrid with their own Poison! I laugh at their impotence, I only ask if I had sent my great works to them for the last 20 years where would have been my name & reputation. In execution & equality [*quality*] of Painting I have never exceeded it, and if it had been placed on the line which by law is fixed as the height for Pictures, no Picture would have had more force.

I have not the least doubt at this critical period, they hoped I would fire up, make a great noise, irritate the Patrons, just before the Cartoon Contest,[3] and so endanger the remaining prospect of my life—I have not complained nor shall I but to you—but it is painful not so much the *power* of doing injury as the intention to try, so visible in Academicians! If you want to see a pure unmitigated specimen of malice, you should look in an Academician's face, when he is *hanging* a *rival!* It is to be raffled for[4] – but I fear this will injure it.

My daughter is still poorly but not worse or sinking – I trust in God.

I fear the Curtius is a bad business – for I get nothing satisfactory about the purchases – Here is a regular Aeschylean croak, like the Daemon in Agamemnon!

So far I have kept up your Spirits – this will be a Contrast!
Yours affectionately<br>B. R. Haydon

*Address:* Miss B. Barrett / 50 Wimpole St.
*Postmark:* MY 12 1843

1. Haydon showed his second painting, "The Assassination of Dentatus," at the Royal Academy's exhibition of 1809. He believed that through the malice of Martin Archer Shee, Thomas Phillips, and Henry Howard, all portrait painters and members of the Academy, the picture was hung in a poorly lit room (*Diary,* I,123).
2. They were called as witnesses by the Select Committee on Arts and Principles of Design in June and July 1836.
3. A contest to choose cartoons from which frescoes would be executed for the new Houses of Parliament.
4. "The Maid of Saragossa" was won by James Webb in a raffle, held on May 23, 1844, which netted Haydon £525.

# 52

---

## *To Miss Barrett*
## *May 16, 1843*

London May 16th 1843

My dearest Friend,

Mary will have done with the first Volume and you shall have it today – I put one note in pencil – my letter to Wilkie on my marriage morn which Cunningham ought to have published—

Harrow on the Hill<br>Oct. 20 1821

My dear Wilkie,

When I swore to die a Batchelor I did not think I should ever live to be a married Man, which I have the inexpressible delight of telling you I became this morning.

Yours ever dear Wilkie<br>B. R. Haydon

Helen told my Sister[1]—he kept walking about all the day with my letter in his hand, saying—"Haydon's married!—dear—dear—Haydon's married!—really!!"

I am hard at work on Alexander & did the arm in a fury yesterday. Is it not a pity that a Man whose whole delight is his Art & family should have anything else to do?

Thanks My dear Friend for this sympathy, but I do hope she will weather it.

Ever yours<br>B. R. Haydon

Your Man departed without waiting—You shall have my memoirs soon—303rd Page—I propose 5 Volumes one after the other. Bentley has answered me & the first move—Speak a good word—I shall make 400 pages each Vol.

I wish to make a guide Book for Artists—*Morally* & *Mentally*—I wish to live in the domestic hearts of my dear Countrymen & Women.

At the Exhibition yesterday I had a high Court—"Are you the Mr. Haydon who painted the Lazarus?"[2]—"Yes Ma'am, I am"—"Dear me, I thought you must be a decrepit old Man"—I bowed—"Ah it is a wonderful Picture—the head of Lazarus. Ah it is wonderful, I always said I never saw such a likeness in all my life to old Col. Carnack of the 17 Dragoons! You are a great Painter Mr. Haydon, indeed you are!"

*Address:* Miss B. Barrett / 50 Wimpole St.
*Postmark:* MY 18 1843

1. Wilkie's sister Helen, who later married Dr. William Hunter, and Haydon's sister Harriett (1789–1884), who married James Haviland in 1815.
2. Haydon painted "The Raising of Lazarus" in 1823.

# 53

*To Miss Barrett
May 16, 1843*

London May 16 1843

My dearest Friend,
    I send you the 1st Volume & the 2nd & many thanks —
                                    Yours truly
                                        B. R. Haydon

*Address:* Miss Barrett / 50 Wimpole St.

# 54

*To Miss Barrett
May 17, 1843*

London May 17th 1843

Dearest Friend,
    When I said *good word* I alluded to *Bentley,* not to *any
public* notice! — & don't suppose I breathe the hundredth
part of a syllable *yet* — no — no, I am no Steam writer for the
season — Why you are a prophet! — how did you know Revelations were coming? — dare I trust *you* with them first? *What*
revelations! — They revived all my early feelings so vividly

I grew sick—they brought before "the inward eye,"[1] the long weary rapturous encumbered struggle! Homer should have placed a Man in Hell as an historical painter in *England!* You know the line[s] in the Odyssey[2]—Sisyphas would have been a joke to him, for torture Ixion & he would have prayed Jupiter to keep them where they were, & at any rate not make them Historical painters *in England!*—

Your Countess on Homer is like Mdle. de Sevigné on Columbus—Avez vous lu, ma chère fille, les voyages de C. Columbe? ils sont très *amusants!*[3] I think it is L'histoire des voyages de C. C. &c. &c.—the greatest discovery on this Earth —a bagatelle for a Court! I go on of course, Journal by Journal, and am got now to 1813—I found a Sketch of Wilkie[4]—painted in 1807—"David Wilkie arguing with some apprehension he will get the worst of it." It is a *gem—exactly like him*—After I have got through the Extracts I will send you the Journal— *in most sacred confidence at present.*

If you go through the life of Wilkie—I think you will like him—in spite of all his quiescent selfishness—He was amiable & affectionate—and when I read [of] his Death (I was at Dover) I felt as if a string was pulled out. I dreamt all night I was at Jerusalem—& visiting with him in the Tombs of the Kings.

Poor Wilkie! you must acknowledge—Women are the grave of Men's Friendships! The moment his Mother & Sister came to Town,[5] away it all went—(our extreme attachment), our "noctes cenaeque Deum"[6] were delightful. Some of his letters to me are delightful as you will say—What a Compound he was! licking the feet of the Nobility, yet he never accepted an Obligation! crying to get a Commission—he stood erect if they offered him an advance!—I found a Drawing of him 1816 which I will send you—get ready the Napoleons, & the Portefeuille—I will send you Fred (Wordsworth's God-Son) & Frank (Sir Walter's)[7]—Mrs. Siddons was to have been his God Mother but she thought it *too solemn* so Mary Mitford was— who was not an Actress—& did not think so—but took it for granted as he [*she*] had so few sins of her own, she had a corner for Frank.

My dearest little Mary I think—is better—

Always yours

B. R. Haydon

*Address:* Miss B. Barrett / 50 Wimpole St.
*Postmark:* MY 18 1843

1. Wordsworth, "I Wandered Lonely as a Cloud," l. 21
2. XI,593–600.
3. In a letter to Mme. de Grignan dated April 1, 1672, Mme. de Sévigné wrote: "Que lisez-vous, ma bonne? Pour moi je lis la découverte des Indes par Christophe Colomb, qui me divertit au dernier point." (What are you reading, my dear? I am reading about the discovery of the Indies by Christopher Columbus, which completely fascinates me. *Lettres de Madame de Sévigné*, ed. Emile Gerard-Gailly [Paris], 1953, Bibliothèque de la Pléïade, I,507).
4. The sketch is reproduced in *Correspondence* (I,252) and in *Lectures* (II,55).
5. They joined Wilkie in London in 1813.
6. Horace, *Satires*, II,vi,65. "Nights and feasts of the gods."
7. Haydon's eldest sons were christened Frank Scott Haydon on July 13, 1829, and Frederic Wordsworth Haydon on September 18, 1840.

# 55

---

## *To Miss Barrett*
## *May 23, 1843*

London May 23 1843

My dearest Friend,

You should consider my notes as a *rattling conversation*— I dont want you to make an anxiety about my auto-da-fe,—is that right? Leave me & the Publishers to fight it out—only you will see it first—*confidentially* of course.

I send you my dear Harry,[1] you shall have all the Haydons on "succession due." On my returned folio, I found a drawing, is it yours or your Sisters? It is very clever — with a slight tendency to *German*. I shall roll my Cartoons to-morrow — there goes Caesar & his Fortunes — Some young monkey will start up, who will swear he drew with his feet. The Town will get mad — & adieu to B. R. Haydon. I shall send you confidentially my *mottoes* in a day or two — you with the subject & a motto *outside* & your name *inside* — if a blank your letter is never opened & there is an end — if a prize it is, & your name is known I do not think the things will be a failure — if they be — it is the duty of Englishmen to *defend* the *first failure*.

Suppose the King of Bavaria had offered prizes to Cornelius [2] for the best specimens of color, impasto, light, shadow, handling? Would not the Germans have failed to a dead Certainty, then why are the English to be taken out of their practice, & expected *at once* to succeed? — Impossibilities are always expected of Inglesi to prove their bottom —

Mind, I consider my own Superb of course —

Yours,<br>B. R. Haydon

*Address:* Miss B. Barrett / 50 Wimpole St.

1. A drawing of Haydon's son Harry, who died in 1834, aged three.
2. Peter von Cornelius (1783–1867), historical painter and dominant figure in German art.

# 56

*To Miss Barrett*
*May 26, 1843*

London May 26 1843

You know Rumohr's Italiensche? [1] — he is a first rate critic — I send you a Sketch of his own —

I am laid up with a burnt foot — in steaming my cartoons

for the last time the Water bubbled out whilst I was looking intensely at it.[2] My Motto on Adam & Eve is, "Desert me not O Lord in my grey hairs, untill I have shewn thy strength unto this generation and thy power unto that which is to come."[3] On Edward: "I called on the Lord out of my low dungeon; thou camest near & said, 'Fear Not.'"[4]

This is confidential.

I have finished the 1st Vol. of my Memoirs, you will read it breathlessly as soon as I have revised it.

Yours ever<br>B. R. Haydon

My kindest regards to Mary Mitford. My daughter is the same—her pulse indicates nothing pulmonary.

*Address:* Miss B. Barrett / 50 Wimpole St.
*Postmark:* MY 26 1843

1. Carl Friedrich Ludwig Felix von Rumohr, *Italiensche Forschungen,* 3 vols., Berlin and Stettin, 1827–1831.
2. The accident occurred on May 20 (*Diary,* V,275).
3. Psalms 71:18. "Now also when I am old and greyheaded, O God, forsake me not; until I have shewed thy strength unto this generation, and thy power to every one that is to come."
4. Lamentations 3:55, 57. "I called upon thy name, O Lord, out of the low dungeon . . . Thou drewest near in the day that I called upon thee: thou saidst, Fear not."

# 57

---

## *To Miss Barrett*
## *May 26, 1843?*[1]

My dear Miss Barrett,

I entrust you with what no human eye but my own has seen—tell me *frankly* your opinion of it, and if it be readable you shall see the rest—

I want the Horse's head & the Friend's head—(the White Horse)—pray consider the manuscript sacredly confidential. I find the journal can't be sent.

Yours

B. R. H.

*Address:* Miss B. Barrett / 50 Wimpole St.

1. This undated letter was probably written on the same day as Letter 56 and a day earlier than Letter 58.

## 58

*To Miss Barrett*
*May 27, 1843*

London May 27 1843

My dearest Friend,

I send you most confidentially the rest of the memoirs— go through carefully & let me send for them Monday—& give me your honest opinion. What a life mine has been!

Acknowledge the receipt & do be careful!! My dear Friend, of fire—not a word at present even to your *Sisters*. Perhaps you ought not to see them, God knows.

B. R. Haydon

*Address:* Miss B. Barrett / 50 Wimpole St.

# 59

---

### *To Haydon*[1]
### *May 27, 1843*

Here is my receipt—I receive the MSS gratefully, & will keep them carefully, & will be silent of them, confidentially —that is, I will not communicate to any human being, father or sister, the things which I shall find therein.

As for the burning—if you hear they are burnt, I myself shall be sure to be in the same funeral pile [*pyre*]. Read & trust—

Your friend<br>Elizabeth B. Barrett

May 27, 1843.

1. This letter, which I now own, was detached from the diary before 1937. It has been sold several times.

# 60

---

### *To Miss Barrett*
### *May 29, 1843*

London May 29 1843

My dearest Friend,

You are a Woman of high poetry of mind & masculine understanding or I would not confidentially have shewn you my life *first*. An ordinary Woman might have been offended to have it sent her unpruned—If you have got through it— your candid opinion—I want—with no reserve.

Yours always,<br>B. R. Haydon

*Address:* Miss B. Barrett / 50 Wimpole St.

# 61

*To Miss Barrett*
*June 1, 1843*

London June 1 1843

My dear Friend,

You are a glorious creature, and another evidence of my *extraordinary sagacity!* — was there ever any thing like it? — here's a Friend I never saw, to whom I have done what I have not done to her I devote my being to, Let her read my Memoirs! — Confide in her honor as if we were twins — & find every thing end exactly as I foresaw it must! if that be not a touch beyond the Mortal what is?

Your letter My dear, is a treasure of sound practical good sense — but dont suppose I have *colored* my Episode, — it is not half up to the reality — a scene which I remember now, is not in — and that is exquisite —

Your Soul is in your remarks — Hazlitt was a perfect fiend! He wrote me with an execution in his House, "Haydon, Esau sold his birthright — I will sell my Louvre copies for a 40 note at 12 months' date" — I went down & gave him a £50 note at a twelvemonth — saved him.

When I was *ruined* — he came & drank tea with us, & looking like a conscious devil, chuckled out with the smile of one just anticipating evil — "I shall get my copies again for nothing." They were bought at my sale under the Sheriff for £4.10 — & he *kept them*[1] — Is that an Angel?

There is nothing you have ever written, has confirmed so intensely my opinion of your power of mind — as *your letter* — I'll be at you when we meet — get well — get well — But do not you see the Namby-Pambyism of the age will never be reformed but by *some blows like my Memoirs*.

My dear Friend, about the Academy you were quite right though public feeling was the strongest — of the three, the whole was a complication.

I have just returned from landing my Cartoons safe & sound
—in Westminster Hall and even to have landed them there
is a triumph. How interesting! who should I see but my own
Pupil Eastlake—Secretary![2]—I said, "Eastlake do you remember taking tea with me 1808, & saying my conversation
fixed you in being a Painter"—"Perfectly," said he—"& Do
you remember coming with me to shew me Westminster
Hall," said Eastlake, "& drawing with the end of your um-
brella a Gigantic limb on the Walls to prove how finely it was
adapted for Painting?"[3]—We were both very much touched
—& think 30 years after I come down with my Cartoons My
Pupil the official to receive the Man to whose instructions he
owes his knowledge! Such is life—
   Pardon Paper.[4]

Ever yours<br>
B. R. Haydon

*Address:* Miss B. Barrett / 50 Wimpole St.

   1. Haydon refers to events of 1819 and 1820 (*Diary*, III,132–133).
   2. Charles Eastlake (1793–1865), later keeper of the National Gallery and
president of the Royal Academy, was at this time secretary to the royal commission on decorating the new Houses of Parliament.
   3. Haydon's diary for June 1, 1843, gives a similar account of taking his
cartoons to the exhibition in Westminster Hall and of his conversation with
Eastlake. He admitted that he did not remember Eastlake's query.
   4. Haydon apologized for finishing his letter on a scrap of paper which
did not match the first two-thirds of it.


# 62

---

*To Miss Barrett*
*June 3, 1843*


London June 3rd 1843

My dear Friend,
   Your remarks are so sound, that I think I shall embody the
whole truth in fictitious names—the object is to shew the

progress of a character – to you the remarks on Aeschylus & Homer may have been read & made 100 years ago but to me they were original[1] – they [were] my young thoughts – you object to them – If I send you the Life again will you draw a pencil line through all you wish out – add nothing only mark – I have begun the second Volume and as I am laid up with a burnt foot, I can only Sketch & write – What think you of a series of *Picturable* illustrations of Britain in Barbarism – Under Roman – Saxon – Danes – Normans – either Picture illustrative of Religion & Law – & heroism & Poetry & music, for Westminster Hall –

Barbarism. Religion, Law, Heroism, Poetry, Music, Art.
Roman. Religion, Election, &c.
Saxon. Religion, &c.
Danes. Religion, &c.
Normans. Religion, &c. Till all was settled.

What a beautiful series might be made of Music for a Music Hall – Discovery for Commercial Hall – Science & Poetry for a Literary Institution – Good God if Power were only given me what I could do! & yet I shall die, & they will go on Painting White lead & mahogany imitations for Centuries if they do not alter – What I fear of this Cartoon affair is – it will be taken up by the Artists as they take up every thing, like a Portrait job a month before the Time! 3 parts of the year they idle – the 3 first months – they work up to the last hour – have all the importance of bustle & no time – send their works wet & half done & think it a great feat! To correct this was the Cartoon affair planned & instead of correcting they have taken it up *in the same trade* light – they are coming at this hour to *me* to ask to see my Steamer! and are only began a fortnight ago!! I really feel disgusted at such disgusting conceit – Such a race as the present of half German, moustashioed, half furred, half clothed, half shaved, half cleaned Dandies make one sick.

The Art Union[2] will raise them like Cabbages to rot on the ground.

Think of Raphael & Michel Angelo taking months about form & correctness & these young Monkies marching up as if to a pas de deux & turn round as they stroke their whiskers, simpering for admiration.

Yours

B. R. Haydon

*Address:* Miss B. Barrett / 50 Wimpole St.
*Postmark:* JU 3 1843

1. Haydon probably referred to this passage in his diary for August 25, 1813: "Are not the greatest works of Genius in the World those where the subject, the power, the material, were equally strong, imposing, & terrific? What is Macbeth? what Agamemnon? what the Iliad? what a stronger exciter than Murder? what than War? And were Shakespeare or Eschylus or Homer considered unpoetic because the very nature of their materials & subjects were per se strong, terrific, exciting? The universal voice of mankind will answer 'certainly not,' because tho their materials were so powerful, yet the greatest skill is required to manage the most powerful materials to prevent them becoming too powerful, to prevent them degenerating into bombast & absurdity" (*Diary*, I,323–324).
2. *The Art-union: A Monthly Journal of the Fine Arts*, first published in February 1839.

# 63

---

*To Miss Barrett*
*June 6, 1843*

London June 6th 1843

I am determined I'll never see you, I am resolved to communicate with an invisibility, our correspondence shall be literally & truly *all Soul!* You ought to be delighted with the imagination! supposing I should leave my manuscripts to you [1] would it not be enchanting to say in the preface—I never saw him—& therefore I can have no partialities—no Friendship, I judge only of his works, & his thoughts—so if you leave yours to me, I can say the same! besides the originality of the Idea is worth something. Tell me whoever thought of such a thing before – and if we meet the other side of the gulph – our minds will feel we are the immortal Two – who in spite of the miserable physical enclosure of body – knew each other only by the Immortal! I maintain its glorious! don't tell for that will spoil it – I am sorry to say, I must descend to mortality, for a twinge in my burnt foot, reminds me the Time is not *yet* come for the *purely* poetical –

I read Vasari, all day – yesterday. Why are Vasari's lives so popular, why have they gone through so many Editions? – because what is anecdotical & human is not sacrificed for the sake of the abstract & professional? why has no modern painter's life ever got to a Second Ed? because the professional is maintained at the expense of the anecdotical – & people get sick of oil & wax – lime, touch, tone & color – naturally enough! The fact that Michel Angelo was liable to head aches is a Comfort, and when I read he had the cramp! – my dear, I rise an inch taller as I walk – admit the genius, but prove to us he was Adam's Son!! – Fuzeli said, "No, you have no business with that" – I used to say we have – I hate your abstract, your Grandisons in Genius – by the bye did you ever read my history of art (Whitakers) I wish you would read it – I sold the copy right, it is 6/- there is an Essay of Hazlitt's attached![2]

50 Cartoons up to last night – I expect 50 more by tomorrow the last day – I fear it will be an *awful sight!*

My dear Sister has sent me a very curious Sonnet to John Haydon[3] an ancestor, author of the Harmoney of the World 1662 – who was fined by Oliver Cromwell 2000 – for siding with the Royal party – I'll *bet he* was an historical painter by the 2000 had it been 20 – & Imprisonment because he *could not pay it* – no further evidence would be wanting of legitimate Ascent –

To the most excellent Philosopher & Lawyer John Haydon upon his so much desired work – Harmoney of the World 1662.

A Public good must quell your private fear,
  The profit of a writer's industry,
Should be imparted to a general Ear
  For Good is bettered by *Community* —
Nor may detraction, or the injury
  Of some men's censures dash what he doth write,
If but what pleaseth all men's sight
  No work could come to light,
  No work should come to light!
Through all the World ye 'ave gather'd the several flowers
  Of other Books into your Harmony
Distill'd to spirit by you they're wholy yours
  So Honey suck'd from the variety
Of Flowers is yet the honey of the Bee
  And tho' in these last days miracles are fled
It brings back time that's past & gives
  Life to the dead.

John Brown, D.D., G.C. Oxon.[4]

Now is that not well done — I have never seen the Book — but will try at the Museum —

I leave you for Vasari — which with Shakespeare, Boswell & Bible are my favourite writers.

Ever yours visible or Invisible,<br>B. R. Haydon

My kind regards to M. Mitford & Miss James. My dear Daughter varies — but is not worse.

*Address:* Miss B. Barrett / 50 Wimpole St.
*Postmark:* JU 6 1843

---

1. At the time of Haydon's suicide three years after he wrote this letter, he hoped that Miss Barrett would edit his autobiography and diary. He had sent all but the last volume of his manuscripts to her. Following the advice of her future husband, she declined to prepare them for publication, and returned the papers to Mrs. Haydon (*Diary,* I,x).

2. *Painting and the Fine Arts,* Edinburgh, 1838. The first of its two articles is by Haydon, the second by Hazlitt; they were reprinted from the seventh edition of the *Encyclopaedia Britannica.*

3. John Heydon was a seventeenth-century astrologer and Rosicrucian, whom Cromwell imprisoned for prophesying that he would be hanged.

4. According to Joseph Foster, only one man named John Brown (1687–1764) received the degree of D.D. (*Alumni Oxoniensis*, Oxford, University of Oxford, 1891, I,195).

# 64

## To Miss Barrett
## June 10, 1843

London June 10 1843

Ah My dear Miss Barrett, you enter into the genius of the thing & your description of my Dear Mother & myself is exquisite – you shall have the rest – & you will be deeply touched – such a Death![1] Good God, after five & thirty years I start up & fancy her dear Influence now near me at this moment – her dear noble generous head, her grand nature – her ambitious urging onward to renown! – her repeated admonition to learn every thing – her devoted fidelity so ill requited by my thoughtless Father – her misery at any of my pains – her anxiety for my happiness – her utter extinction of self, dear noble Creature – I have the delight of knowing I spent my first earnings – £60 – to bury her where she wished at Ide, the living her Father had – She was born to the grave by an old tenant, who remembered Miss Sally in her Youth! & wept over her – Good God, all this has been out of my head for years but always in my heart – & now at midnight when I write it, I start & feel a large tear hanging & not dropping by the weight of its own intensity –

I send you the rest with equal confidence & will go on with the whole – if you think it is right –

Ever & ever yours
B. R. Haydon

There are moments worthy of Immortality & these are they!

*Address:* Miss B. Barrett / 50 Wimpole St.

1. During Haydon's visit to his parents in Plymouth in 1807, three years after he had gone to London to become an artist, his mother developed angina pectoris. He and his sister started to take her to London to consult a specialist, but en route she died at an inn (*Autobiography*, I,58–63).

# 65

## *To Miss Barrett*
## *June 18, 1843*

London June 18 1843

My sweet Unseen,

I daresay you will be very angry at such a liberty – but consider if after six months writing I am not entitled to the distinction of being allowed it.

What are you about? & when am I to see you? The weather is settled, & every thing contributing to render your recovery secure.

On dit there [are] 170 Cartoons! A Commissioner told me about 30 were an honor to the Country – that the Prince was astonished at the Genius & power of historical composition displayed. Have I not always said so? Give them a higher demand & you will have works equal to it. Most of these productions have been executed by young Men who have been getting a scanty living by doing any thing for any body, & perhaps instead of being encouraged to persevere will be allowed to sink back again to do any thing for any body, that they may not starve. I hope not – If properly wielded into a road for regular devellopement the Genius of England will come forth in majesty & power, but if frittered away in a parcel of disjointed Efforts without plan or principle I foresee the result. The curse of the Nation is *a hatred of any superi ority* – Wealth, rank, Genius or Monarch.

My dear Child is varying but no cough – What a dear sweet girl! – do you know when I pray for her recovery it sticks in my throat [1] – I felt in that dreary but poetical hour (the interval hour between midnight & day break) as if she was too pure to be allowed to remain! – God knows – I could not pray with the ardor I always do for My Ambition!

We go to Harrow today to see Byron's Tombstone[2] & autograph – & to amuse her, as she reads him with such interest.

Harrow I went [to] at my marriage – & it has many of my earlier associations –

God bless you<br>B. R. Haydon

What do you think of putting Journal in as Appendix – altogether?

*Address:* Miss B. Barrett / 50 Wimpole St.
*Postmark:* JU 19 1843

1. *Macbeth*, II,iii,32–33. "I had most need of blessing, and 'Amen' / Stuck in my throat."
2. The grave of John Peachey, known as Byron's tomb. It was a favorite spot of the poet while he was a student at Harrow. He referred to it in "On a Distant View of the Village and School of Harrow on the Hill": "Again I behold where for hours I have ponder'd, / As reclining, at eve, on yon tombstone I lay" (ll. 13–14).

# 66

*To Miss Barrett*
*June 19, 1843*

London June 19 1843

My dearest Friend,

We visited Harrow yesterday, saw his autograph lately discovered in repairing the gallery – & another also – like this in pencil – Byron. We stood on the grave of his Allegra[1] – & sat on Peachey's tomb where he used to lounge – 4 more enthusiastic admirers – or 4 more informed & read in his writings, never pilgrimized before – the Day was Unfavorable – but I think of Painting (in his Youth) Byron musing on this

Spot[2]—I have an original Water color drawing of Lady C. Lamb of him swimming with Boatswain,[3] left by her at her Lodgings & come to us lineally & regularly & accidentally—you shall see it—

We drew up at a little bye Inn, on a Woody & bye road, & on enquiring if they had a meadow behind, & would grant us chairs & table—they had—out we all got—& carrying our provisions into the meadow, Frank (1st prizeman), My dear Daughter & my dear Mary & I laid the cloth, & dined in sun shine buried in grass cooled by Shadow, & scenting of Hay, our *Coldstream* band were the sweet innocent joyous birds which sang round us, with a fluttering chirrup, that was delightful—In the midst however was the usual Evil. My sweetest Daughter, pathetic, suffering, pale & beautiful face —I never saw her look so handsome, & was not aware how heavenly disease etherialises the human face! Good God, what a look! her large dark blue eyes, her exquisite full trembling nose, her pouting red lips, her oval shaped cheeks, fine forehead, & beautiful chin—her arched brows quivering with suppressed feeling, & her lustrous glance at all of us, as if she thought of leaving us, went to my very heart's core! I am obliged to suppress my feelings for Her sake—But Mary & I dare not be *alone*—for with us there is no concealment—Frank is dreadfully touched, & has got quiet, & said he felt giddy, when he saw her—The Howe is expected Home every day & Frederick will break his sailor's heart when he sees her.

It really is very hard not to preserve one daughter out of three—but we have been so accustomed to Calamity, and she, the love, has seen so little else, but Insult & degradation to me, & shared them so long, that it is my opinion the dread of the future has brought it on more than other things.

I hold such eternal intercourse with "Him who is invisible"[4] that nothing in life can shake me more, and as to the Cartoons, My dearest Friend, I expect the usual attempt to lower my rank in the hearts of the people, and its usual success—they do not occupy a thought—I did them as a duty to my Country, & to aid the opposition to that unnatural party, who have no belief in the Genius of England, & wish to bring in the talented but mistaken Germans – Hess & Kaulbach are now seen at the British Gallery, by the side of Reynolds, *they* have found as Handlers of the Brush their proper line, two or three such Comparisons will settle the question – or it is settled already.

I perceive a nasty, envious, malicious feeling – about me, I fear to enquire. There exists a conviction that God Almighty has no right to be guilty of the impertinence of gifting Genius; without a Ministerial Majority of the House, sanctioned by the Lords, signed by the Crown & sealed by the Chancellor! –

The dignity of Aristocracy is offended! – Authority gets stiff! – Already there are hints – the Cartoons are so *nearly* equal – It will puzzle them – *No,* they are not puzzled at all! – They have made up their minds! – & under the pretence of equality of talent shelter their determination to assassinate. We shall see – I expect nothing – To distinguish between what is bad & what is good falls to the lot of many – but to distinguish between what is very good, and what is truly excellent falls to the lot of few – says Burke – & those few are not likely to be Kings & Princes.

In the mean time I am & shall remain dead quiet – & trust in God I shall have health to produce Works enough by Next Year to fling myself with my usual defiance before the World alone & free: that is my element – in association I do not feel at home – "What matter where if *I* be still the same."[5] I only hope I shall die at the right time, *the* time I have made the greatest Impression.

I move Curtius today, to the usual Dust hole in Dean St. where hangs Solomon, my *first* large & now *last* large Work – Honor to the Patrons of Britain! I sold it to a poor Devil, who has more taste than money, & won't let it go till he pays. Addio –

Yours affectionately,
B. R. Haydon

*Address:* Miss B. Barrett / 50 Wimpole St.
*Postmark:* JU 20 1843

1. Allegra, daughter of Byron and Claire Clairmont, died in 1822 at the age of five and is buried at the entrance of Harrow Church.
2. Haydon began "Byron Musing on a Distant View of Harrow" on September 15, 1845, but never finished the painting.
3. Byron's Newfoundland dog.
4. Hebrews, 11:27. "For he endured, as seeing him who is invisible."
5. *Paradise Lost*, I,256.

# 67

## *To Haydon*
*about June 20, 1843* [1]

must of course be regulated by the individual character, by his degree of strength of mind & serenity, — & very carefully regulated in such cases as the actual one, where to keep the spirits free from all agitation is so necessary to recovery. Would she not bear to hear that her lungs are considered delicate? Would *that* frighten her?

I fear, this will be a dreadful anxiety to poor Mrs. Haydon. She is your only daughter, — is she not? and very beautiful? like her mother? Has she been long ill?

Try to take courage and hope! — and may God bless you in His will! —

Ever faithfully yours<br>E. B. B.

Miss Mitford shall hear — I am none the worse except by a bad night for my laborious day yesterday.

1. Only the last page of this letter survives. It cannot be dated with certainty but clearly refers to the illness of Haydon's daughter, referred to in letters of this period. Professor Shackford, who had not seen Haydon's letters, dated this fragment "[Aug.–Oct. 1843?]," since he alluded to his daughter's illness in his diary of August 15, 1843.

# 68

---

*To Miss Barrett
June 22, 1843*

London June 22 1843

I forgot to tell you, I never published these notices of Leigh Hunt — I meant to have done it, but remembering I could only have acquired my knowledge by intimacy I considered it dishonorable — they have remained ever since in my drawer — & by accident I found them. Return them to me as soon as Convenient & when I send Byron let me have Wilkie —

I have been hard at Alexander all day — Adieu —

B. R. Haydon

Lord Morpeth made a very fine Speech yesterday at the Anti-Slavery meeting.

*Address:* Miss B. Barrett / 50 Wimpole St.
*Postmark:* JU 23 1843

# 69

---

*To Miss Barrett
June 27, 1843?*[1]

Confidential
Dearest Friend,

Please to take care of these books for me — May I entrust a Chest of private Papers — a large chest for a time —

*As I predicted — My Cartoons have no reward* — particulars as soon as I can — only send up an answer as soon as convenient — a note — leave it without waiting.

Yours ever,
B. R. Haydon

*Address:* Miss B. Barrett / 50 Wimpole St.

1. This letter was almost certainly written soon after Haydon received Eastlake's letter of June 27, 1843, informing him that his "drawings are not included among those that have been rewarded" in the cartoon competition (*Diary*, V,293).

# 70

## *To Miss Barrett*
## *June 28, 1843*

London June 28 1843

My dearest Friend,

I consign to your care my chest of private papers – take care of them for God's sake.

I shall send also two Jars of valuable oil to me which might be placed in the Wine Cellar.

Many many thanks –

I send for you a bit of Napoleon willow.

Yours ever<br>B. R. Haydon

*Address:* Miss B. Barrett / 50 Wimpole St.

# 71

## *To Miss Barrett*
## *June 29, 1843*

London June 29 1843

Pray My dearest Friend Distinctly understand there is nothing in the box but papers & books & letters –

The oil is precious – & I have sent you nothing but what it is honorable to entrust to your care [1] –

I am ruined depend on it, by this decision & can only trust you will entirely recover in a short time – Weakness is never dangerous, after so long a time.

Yours ever<br>B. R. Haydon

*Address:* Miss B. Barrett / 50 Wimpole St.

1. Haydon wrote in his diary for July 1, 1843: "A Day of great misery. I said to my dear love, 'I am not included!' Her expression was a study! She said, 'We shall be ruined.' I locked up my lectures, papers, & Journals, & sent them to my dear Aeschylus Barrett with two jars of oil (1816), 27 years old. I burnt loads of private letters, & prepared for executions" (*Diary*, V,294). See Letters 69 and 70.

# 72

---

*To Haydon*
*July 2, 1843*

July 2, 1843

My dear friend

I return your letter according to your desire – but I see *through my fears,* & do beseech you to pause & consider the circumstances, before you give your heart to the public or indicate it by a gesture, on the present occasion. It will be said of you, "because he is a disappointed man, he speaks as an angry man." You will have less influence, & a dishonor will be done, beyond what an enemy could effect alone, upon the dignity of your position.

Forgive me! It is my interest for you that is insolent in my words to you! If you can "cheer in the Hall" – cheer to be a Spartan in your exultation! – but a hiss or a sneer from your lips at the actual moment, may be caught up & retorted.

Ever faithfully yours<br>Elizabeth B. Barrett

Do tell me exactly what you think of the cartoons. I shall be impatient to hear. Did you return to me the third volume of Wilkie? I think not. Have you done with it—& may I have it?

1. Like Letter 59, this letter, which I now own, was detached from the diary before 1937. It has been sold several times.

# 73

---

### To Miss Barrett
### July 3, 1843

London July 3rd 1843

My dear Friend,

I am as much the Spartan & Lion as ever but in this case it is necessary to be a little of the Carthaginian.

The possibility of a half dozen Executions is a possibility which would have made a Spartan take care of his papers, especially if he had such a Friend as you—So no more on that subject.

I have been to day—& am perfectly satisfied—the display is an honor to the Country & I keep my position—Whatever the press puts forth there is no Country in Europe could at a Call have made such an effort—the young men rallied round me in a way which was delightful.

The only errors in decision of the chosen are two—Parris [1]— & Armitage,[2] a pupil of De la Roche, though skilfully & artistically managed, the drawing & anatomy for which the French consider themselves celebrated are such that no boy in my school should have remained a week—who knew no more of the figure.

I am literally astonished at the impudence in the Youth & ignorance of the Deciders [3] & it comes to the usual conclusion, which I told them at Oxford, that unless they have professors of Art, the nobility will never be able to judge of what is good

& what is bad—in such matters—I shall give the University a second course on such subjects—

The Death of Lear[4]—Alfred in the Danish Camp[5]—are extremely fine, & worthy of any period of Art. Boadicea by Seilous,[6] Caractatus by Watts,[7] full of Genius,—Watts has a 300 prize—Seilous has only a hundred, when it ought to have been 300. In fact I never saw such neglect of what is fine. Seilous' hundred ought to be given to Armitage, & his 300 to Seilous.

The Cant of believing they would commit themselves if a deference was not paid to something from a French atelier, is exquisite!—The Queen was told this Boy was only 22— but she was not told of an English boy of 16—who has an interior of the plague[8]—exceedingly full of expression & pathos—

You are decidedly right in not sending the letter yet—but you need not fear me—I will do nothing—& remember, I have nothing to do with any thing directly or indirectly, which may appear in the Press & that I do nothing without my name—Ever—

You are a dear Friend & keep your mind easy—

B. R. Haydon

*Address:* Miss B. Barrett / 50 Wimpole St.

1. Edmund Thomas Parris (1793–1873) won a prize of £100 for "Joseph of Arimathaea Converting the Britons."
2. Edward Armitage (1817–1896) won a prize of £300 for "Caesar's First Invasion of Britain."
3. The Judges of the competition were Sir Robert Peel, Lord Landsdowne, Samuel Rogers, Sir Richard Westmacott, Richard Cook, and William Etty.
4. By Frederick Richard Pickersgill (1820–1900).
5. By Marshall Claxton (1813–1868).
6. Henry Courtney Selous (1811–1890) won a prize of £100.
7. George Frederick Watts (1817–1904) won a prize of £300 for "Caractacus Led in Triumph through the Streets of Rome."
8. Probably E. Corbould's "The Plague of London, A.D. 1349." The bishops and clergy are represented at St. Paul's-cross praying for the cessation of the pestilence" (*The Athenaeum,* July 22, 1843, p. 674). But Edward Henry Corbould was twenty-eight at the time of this contest. He received a prize for his "Pest in London" (Ulrich Thieme and Felix Becker, *Allgemeines Lexikon der bildenden Künstler von der Antike bis zur Gegenwart,* 36 vols., Leipzig, Verlag von E. A. Seemann, 1911–1947, VII,395).

# 74

London July 11 1843

My dearest Friend,

What is become of you?

What have you heard of the Cartoons? – Am I cut up? – When am I to be presented in form? Not till you come into the drawing room.

My daughter says this day is horrible, Winter was not worse – Will you write me you have received a chest of Private papers to be delivered at my order.

Have you heard from Mary Mitford – Do let me hear of you.

Ever yours faithfully

B. R. Haydon

*Address:* Miss B. Barrett / 50 Wimpole St.
*Postmark:* JY 12 1843

# 75

*To Miss Barrett*
*July 13, 1843*

London July 13th 1843

My dearest Friend,

My Cartoons are 33 & 118 – You see, I have been active – & pushing the Commission on to do the whole thing with honor –

The plan of private day, Queen,[1] &c., was all mine laid before them in March & being *unofficial* – I think they thought

London July 13th
1843

My dearest Friend, my Cartoons
are 33 — & 118 —
you see, I have been active —
& pushing the Commission on
to do the which they will
honor —
The Plan of private day,
Queen, &c were all some
laid before them in march
& being unofficial — I heard
they thought I dictated —
again I fear, the diplomacy
of Eastlake — He knows the
hold I have — of the public
& he wants to weaken it —
I don't fear me — Nelson sealing
the Letter at Copenhagen &
rubbed in — & Alexander settled
B R Haydon

I *dictated* – Again I fear the diplomacy of Eastlake – he knows the hold I have of the public & he wants to weaken it – Don't fear me – Nelson sealing the letter at Copenhagen is rubbed in & Alexander settled.

B. R. Haydon

1. "The Queen and Prince Albert, and the King and Queen of the Belgians, went yesterday to inspect the Cartoons in Westminster-hall, attended by the Royal Suite" (*The Times,* July 1, 1843, p. 7).

# 76

*To Miss Barrett*
*July 15, 1843*

London July 15 1843

My dearest Friend,

You seemed to [be] alarmed for *my fate* – the most promising Cartoons & finished Academy drawings generally end in producing the most *wretched painters* – We know this & await – The most unpretending Cartoons announce generally a Capability of the Brush. These are Artistical distinctions practice only can give – therefore be you easy as to ultimate results. What I have to dread is the hatred of Peel & treachery of Eastlake – between them there is no hope for me, that rely on.

But, I can wield the public heart – & the public now are asking for my opinion – at a proper time they shall have it – & I am hard at work but my fate is the *hair* of Damocles!

Yours most truly<br>B. R. Haydon

Howard, Chalon, Hart, Geddes, Patten are the Academy members.[1]

*Address:* Miss B. Barrett / 50 Wimpole St.
*Postmark:* JY 15 1843

# 77

*To Miss Barrett*
*July 18, 1843*

London July 18 1843

My dear Friend,

I think as highly as any body can do of Cope's Jury,[1] but I heartily despise the landing of Caesar[2] – it has nothing but impudent execution without knowledge, or real skill & will end in smoke.

I see clearly enough you do not believe in the grounds of my belief, that my enemies have taken advantage to lower my hold of the public heart (if they can) by their iniquitous decision. Faults I have in abundance of course, & one great one is my love of the Truth, which I have stuck to, and will ever, to the end of my Life; they don't like my public assumption of the right to dictate from long experience, & intense study from having educated the most eminent men of the day – I can prove that Edward & John are entitled to the highest honor for Character & expression, the one for sorrow & submissive "abandon," the other for mastering his glorying in the hour of Triumph with the delicacy & breeding of a Prince, reigning in an ambling poney, with the grace & skill of a Horseman! – & a Hero[3] –

Now you have my opinion of my own work, and who does not feel & see these things is wilfully blind, or callously obtuse, & is to be pitied.

I'll bide my time, but if God spare my intellect & eyes, I'll carry desolation & dissection into the hearts of those who have wantonly dishonored me; after such a battle as I have fought, & such tortures as I have endured, for the Truth: we'll see if I can't move the public again as I have done before – so look ahead as the Americans say for as sure as you are a sweet & delicate adviser I'll do it.

Ever thine truly,<br>B. R. Haydon

*Private.* Mary Mitford's note is sufficiently cold, as I fear mine was about her affairs –

P.S. I relinquish all hope of the houses or having any thing to do with them – so you see I know my path.

*Address:* Miss B. Barrett / 50 Wimpole St.

1. Charles West Cope (1811–1890) exhibited his cartoon "The First Trial by Jury."
2. See Letter 73, note 2.
3. Haydon alluded to his cartoon "The Black Prince Entering London in Triumph" (see Letter 16).

# 78

---

## To Miss Barrett
## July, 18, 1843

London July 18 1843

Now My dearest Friend,

I hope you are convinced now, my convictions are founded.

The second decision is more ridiculous than the first, per fectly ridiculous, and I am again left out,[1] as a Marked Man, I told you so – the Court hate me because I oppose the Germans – the Academy because I brought them before a Committee – and Sir Robert because I perpetually put him in mind of his duty to the Art. The Artists join & Society back the Artists but I defy them all – if the people stand by me, for whose information I have devoted my life.

I never felt better—you know I was prepared for this—you know what I said.

I am only wounded at the Cruelty of my Species & its hatred of Truth.

I am dearest Friend<br>B. R. Haydon

*Address:* Miss B. Barrett / 50 Wimpole Street
*Postmark:* JY 18 1843

1. "We understand that the Commissioners on the Fine Arts have selected ten additional Cartoons as worthy each of a reward (prize, we presume, it cannot be called) of 100*l.*, and that the artists are Messrs. Pickersgill, Corbauld, Howard, R.A., W. C. Thomas, Stephanoff, Claxton, F. Howard, Rippingille, J. C. Waller, and Sir W. Ross, R.A." (*The Athenaeum,* July 15, 1843, p. 652).

# 79

---

## To Haydon
## *July [19,] 1843*

July—Wednesday—

Indeed my dear friend, you judge me wrong if you doubt of the extent & fulness of the sympathy with which I have followed you in loss and disappointment. If I am unwilling to believe in persecution & treachery *that* is a natural unwillingness, I think, both for your sake & the world's. I am unwilling to think so ill of Eastlake in particular as would stamp him a traitor.[1] And I thought it possible—perhaps I think so still—that the sensitiveness which belongs to your temperament & which expresses itself so often in a generous vehemence for good or against evil, may have betrayed you on this occasion into a bitterness of personal reflection you would be eager to modify one year afterwards. I am judging coldly, you think perhaps, while you are suffering poignantly.

True – I am judging – *not coldly* – because indeed I do not feel coldly – but with the degree of dispassionateness which an acquaintance with the facts apart from an acquaintance with the actors, (*you* being rather a sufferer than an actor!) would necessarily leave to me – and it is simply on this ground that the possibility rests, of my being nearer the truth than you are yourself.

Now try to forgive me for not being sure of the existence of this conspiracy against you. I am used, you know, to hold that occasional adversities, failures, & misconceptions are evils in the way of a noble ambition, & that the world throws stones before the feet of such an ambition, instead of gravelling her path. Your late disappointment is a very bitter one – I can enter painfully into the whole bitterness of it – but it is not worse than other men of genius have sustained, & risen higher in consequence of. When Corinna took the crown from over Pindar's head,[2] all Greece looking on, he was mortified & grieved of course – but he did not upbraid his judges with treachery – and who speaks now of Corinna? Wordsworth, all the reviewers & three quarters of the public laughed to scorn[3] as an inarticulate idiot; but he upbraided none of them with conspiracy, and who scorns Wordsworth now?

Commissioner-prizes & academical crowns have been given since the world began to feeble hands & narrow foreheads – because the strong hand & broad brow can afford to *wait* while the ignorant learn to measure them – not so much because there is malice in the world, as because there is ignorance. What poem is estimated aright in this world of ours? There is over-praise or there is under-praise – there is seldom indeed a full & correct appreciation. And yet of what use would it be; nay, what vain & mad extremity of impatience would it be, if every poet who considered himself depreciated by either the public or the critics, cried aloud as a wronged man, accusing his fellow-men of personal malignity towards him? Is not the noble way for the poet, to destroy his critic by *more poems* instead of by critical pamphlets? I think so. I should aspire towards such a vengeance myself. And yet it is very hard as even *I* have felt, to bear silently unjust judgments founded sometimes upon a mistake in matters of the fact. The critics have been goodnatured to me in my unimportance, as far as might be expected of critics: and yet even *I* have felt it hard. To some persons, it must be peculiarly hard & oppressive, — and they are nevertheless *silent*.

Now I think that all producers of works of art, whether musical composers, painters or poets, are subjected to the same occasional adversities from the fluctuation of the rank popular breath: & what they have all to fall back on, or rather to stand up by, is self-reliance & intensity of purpose. I rather doubt whether they have any right to reproach their critics for mistakes which have resulted from a critical ignorance & not from a social malice — but assuredly they can have no wisdom in making public such a reproach, & little dignity.

And with regard to these cartoons, having seen nothing at all of them, I cannot, you know, be sure whether justice or injustice has been done in the decision, however great may be my own regret & disappointment at it. You are a man of genius — but you may have failed in the cartoons — in these particular cartoons; with all your genius — and it is impossible for one who is most your friend to deny the hypothesis of it. On the other hand, you may not have failed — your cartoons may deserve the first prizes; & you may be a cruelly wronged man. Still *a mistake* may have wronged you, & not a treachery — and you cannot deny the possibility of this. It is better & happier to doubt of the knowledge of men than of their integrity — and it is for your own sake that I press this consideration upon you. Mr. Lucas called your cartoon of Adam & Eve "sublime work" — I had never doubted for a moment your gaining one prize at least — and I understand, I repeat, to the uttermost the anguish of the re-action of your aspiration. But think — if you were to write violently! if you were to speak violently to another besides me! I beseech you — pause —

A little forbearance — and you may have work in the Houses of Parliament — a rest for the sole of the foot of your genius within the walls of the Legislature. I hope earnestly so.

How can our dear friend have expressed herself "coldly"? I am sure you were never "cold to her" — and "I would not hear your enemy say so:"[4] nor would *she* say so, who is your friend! — She has often & anxiously spoken of you to me — coldly never! — and you should consider that if she speaks little of the cartoons, she has seen none of them — and that *further to excite your sensitive feelings by violent words, would not be the part of a friend, in either herself or me.* I have said very little to her on the subject — & nothing in regard to *deposits* — to be more worthy of your confidence: but you must not on that account my dear friend reproach either of us with coldness — I can scarcely believe such a word of *her!* —

Most faithfully yours<br>Elizabeth B. Barrett

After all there may be injustice — by favoritism towards others, not malice towards you! — The Academicians have come in for the recompensing codicil of hundreds, I see.[5]

1. See Letter 76.
2. "Corinna was said to have been Pindar's teacher. She gained a victory over him in a verse contest at Thebes. In Landor's 'Southey and Porson,' Miss Barrett had perhaps read that Pindar was defeated by Corinna five times" (Shackford, p. 72).
3. *Macbeth*, V,vii,12. "But swords I smile at, weapons laugh to scorn."
4. *Hamlet*, I,ii,170.
5. See Letter 78, note 1.

# *80*

---

*To Miss Barrett*
*July 19, 1843*

July 19th 1843

My dear Intellectual,

Alexander gets on — if I get over this week well, I shall send for my Papers again.

Be assured of my discretion only I *know* more than you possibly can.

Ever yours<br>B. R. Haydon

Wilkie's 2nd is still here. See Civil Engineer Journal of this month.[1]

1. Haydon reviewed Cunningham's *Life of Sir David Wilkie* in the *Civil Engineer and Architect's Journal* of July 1843 (6:226).

## *81*

*To Miss Barrett*
*July 20, 1843*

London July 20th 1843

My dear Friend,

So you think the predominant vice of humanity is not *hatred* of superiority—that when a Young Man was persecuted for his zeal in early life & successfully resisted it, there could not remain any desire in his persecutors to catch him if they could in his maturity, & give a gripe that should make him remember; now as I know the World better than you, pray pardon me.

Before you were born the old cry of Conspiracy was raised against me—I do not believe in any conspiracy for I believe them to be such rascals they would be afraid of each other to conspire. But I believe Power to be so Detestably revengeful that dancing in the ashes of an enemy would only wet its appetite.

I have got into a scrape by my Arder,—by the way do you know the Life of Henry Arder,[1] a Friend of mine, a capital Life—shall I send it? Can you send me your Epic—I never saw any Miniatures of Miss Gillies[2]—

Do not you think I am so weak as to believe in a conspiracy. I am only perfectly sure my Cartoons are fine things, & that the Judges must have remembered to forget them.

Yours &c.,

B. R. Haydon

Tell me when it would not be an annoyance to you & the family to send for my box—Many thanks for protecting it—& my Immortal Jars.

*Address:* Miss B. Barrett / 50 Wimpole St.
*Postmark:* JY 21 1843

1. Colbert Kearney, Esq., identified Henry Ardor as the subject of an essay entitled "The Cartoons—1819, 1843" in *The Civil Engineer and Architect's Journal* of August 1843 (pp. 274-277). The essay is unsigned but obviously was written by Haydon, for all biographical details of Ardor except his death are identical with Haydon's. On successfully sponsoring a cartoon competition for decorating the new Houses of Parliament, Ardor died happily at fifty-seven, the precise age of Haydon when he wrote the essay. See Appendix A.

2. Margaret Gillies (1803–1887), portrait painter and miniaturist.

# 82

## *To Haydon*
## *about July 21, 1843*

Friday morning

My dear Mr. Haydon,

I willingly make the admissions you insist upon. I know very little of the world;—scarcely anything in a social sense—and except as one judges of without, from within. I admit moreover that an opposition to all superiority,—is perhaps a hatred of it,—is of the world, worldly.

Whenever you like to send for the boxes, you can have them; and for one reason I shall be very glad to lose the guardianship of them & of the "immortal oils." May the last flow onward like Aaron's oils—from the head to the skirts of the garment![1]—

Your Mr. Foggo's[2] modesty does really amuse me. Thank you for letting me see his catalogue,—which I return to you with the other, lent before. The judgments run against the decision of the commissioners both here I observe, & out of doors I understand.

Keep Orion.[3] You are epical enough yourself to care for epics!—

Ever faithfully yours
Elizabeth B. Barrett

Long live Alexander!—May he be strong and prevail!—

Do you mean to say that Wilkie's Life, the second volume of it I mean;—is still with you? If so, & you have done with it, will you let the bearer have it? I shall fall into the lion's den, should the bookseller discover that I have not returned it to him.

Thank you much for the sight of Napoleon's relic, which is herewith returned.[4]

---

1. Psalms, 133:2. "It is like the precious ointment upon the head, that ran down upon the beard, even Aaron's beard: that went down to the skirts of his garments."

2. The Foggo brothers, James (1789–1860) and George (1793–1869), collaborated in historical paintings and lithographs.

3. Richard Henry Horne's *Orion* (London, J. Miller, 1843). "Horne fixed the price of the first three editions at a farthing a copy—sold only to those who pronounced the name with accent on the penult. Mrs. Browning's review of the poem appeared in *The Athenaeum*, June 24, 1843" (Shackford, p. 73).

4. See Letter 70.

# 83

*To Miss Barrett*
*July 28, 1843*

London July 28 1843

My dear Friend,

How a Man of my experience in the World & Society & all the separate Classes I had offended by my love of Art & love of Truth could be so weak as to put myself in their power is one of those anomalies the Weakest & wisest are sometimes guilty of.

The Connoiseurs have never forgot their prostration on the Elgin Marbles,[1] the Academicians their whitened exasperation before the Committee[2] — nor the Nobility my lectures at Oxford on their imperfect knowledge of Art.[3]

These 3 classes were my judges, & they have well paid me off my old score in hopes I [am] so old as not to bear these oppressions as I did in my Youth — am I? Maturity is better able to bear than Youth. I send you some more Books to guard, if not a liberty —

I had a kind letter from Lockart[4] yesterday, who feels severely my treatment, he says what is the Truth, Caractacus, The Jury & Edward the Black Prince ought to have been the 3 first. This is exactly my own honest conviction.

Be assured my dear Friend, people are annoyed at the display of talent — more than pleased and instead of employing these young men under direction, mine or others, they will let them sink back again to get their daily bread. You saw what Brougham said, after all — The Building Committee might prevent the thing going further or the Wisdom of Parliament![5]

This is what I foresaw, my restless urging is a nuisance they don't like — & the enthusiasm of the people is so exactly what I told them it would be that they are frightened at what I shall urge them next. Poor Creatures, unworthy the people accident has placed beneath them.

God bless you

Ever yours

B. R. Haydon

Fred is paid off from the Howe & re-appointed to the Penelope & was home for a week—much improved he went this morning—& thank God he did so from a home of harrass & daily expectation of a Gaol—depend on it that is a fact & don't you be astonished when it comes.

*Address:* Miss B. Barrett / 50 Wimpole St.

1. Haydon's pamphlet *The Judgment of Connoisseurs* (reprinted from *The Examiner* of March 17, 1816) attacked connoisseurs, particularly Payne Knight, for their failure to appreciate the Elgin Marbles.
2. On July 16, 1836, Haydon testified before a committee of Parliament investigating the Royal Academy.
3. Haydon delivered six lectures at Oxford in March 1840.
4. John Gibson Lockhart (1794–1854), editor of the *Quarterly Review* from 1825 to 1853, son-in-law and biographer of Sir Walter Scott.
5. Haydon wrote in his diary for July 25, 1843: "'After the models were sent in, it by no means followed employment would follow because the *wisdom* of Parliament might refuse to carry it further.' Lord Brougham, July 25, 1843." On the word *wisdom* he wrote a footnote, "Ignorance" (*Diary*, V,298).

# 84

---

## To Miss Barrett
### July 29, 1843

London July 29th 1843

My dear Friend,

I have given vent in a lecture which I shall deliver as soon as possible—

Depend on it, my treatment has been infamous. After it is delivered you shall see it—& depend on it, my Cartoons are on the Italian not the German principle—I shall exhibit an exquisite carto[o]n by Raphael—a Picture in Charcoal—& prove all I wish.

Yours always<br>B. R. Haydon

Take care of my Paradise regained—

*Address:* Miss B. Barrett / 50 Wimpole St.
*Postmark:* JY 31 1843

# 85

*To Miss Barrett*
*August 8, 1843*

London Aug 8 1843

My dearest Dream,

You are an imagination to me!—& I like it.

I gave my lecture last night to a crowded & enthusiastic audience!—I wish you had been there—I had an exquisite Cartoon by Raffael, & proved to the Audience the superiority of the Italian to the German Cartoon—My Cartoons tend to the Italian & not the German & the German being the go at Court, I had no chance—I send you the lecture, & will send for it tomorrow morning, take care of it—& will send also for my box—

Though hideously pressed I have escaped the immediate danger of executions!—how *mysteriously* have I been influenced all my Life!—About an hour before going last night I mounted to my Heavenly Study—& felt as if conversing with a Supernatural being!—all my life crowded to my mind! I thought here now is another Crisis, failure would be perpetual ridicule!—if I fail—but why should I—have I not always had a brilliant beam in my brain, with "go on" in a star, shining in the midst—Have I not often heard awful

Whispers as if from some Awful Spirit! In the storm &
thunder does not my Soul feel, as if I was a part of the turbulence! I cannot have been urged on in this way, to be destroyed
& marked! – no – I shall succeed, & let no doubts torment me.
There lay the Bible before me. Shall I open & consult the
lots – Why? – I must – & I did & descended to go, cool &
collected –

My Beautiful Heroine of a Mary with her rich exquisite face
was there & my second Son & they witnessed the Completest
Victory of any lecture I ever gave – full of their aspirations I
was of course cheated by my money taker & *this is life!*

Adieu – the lecture is private for you – and if not very
troublesome – may I have the box *today?*

God bless you

Ever yours & ever

B. R. Haydon

When I talk of *my affairs* remember it is to *unburthen* not
to excite *sympathy* or *assistance* – I like to relieve my mind.

Address: Miss B. Barrett / 50 Wimpole St.

## 86

*To Miss Barrett*
*August 10, 1843*

London Aug 10 1843

My dearest Friend

Have you done with my lecture? – and what do you think
of it?

Yours truly

B. R. H.

Fishing!

*Address:* Miss B. Barrett / 50 Wimpole St.

# 87

*To Miss Barrett*
*August 16, 1843*

London Aug 16 1843

My Dream!

If you want to enjoy Windsor Castle, I will tell you how to do —

Take the Testament in your pocket — go to Herne's Oak, stretch yourself out & read St. Paul! — Every now & then look up, & perhaps you will see a little glittering speck in a little hole, in a long Stone Castle with Turrets, that's the Queen! — then you will see a dozen specks come galloping down with little bits of yellow cases on wheels — they are (specks & cases) the Royal family. Then you will look again & call to mind, in that long stone looking turretted Prison, how all these little specks eat, drink, sleep, pray, blow their little noses, wash their little faces, some have got corns on their little toes — some pimples on their little chins — & two of the specks strut, very upright, & say they are the Lord's anointed! — but if their teeth ake, they cry out — if they have indigestion — they send for a Doctor — & make wry faces & drink nasty stuff — they have feet so cramped, they can hardly walk because tight shoes are the fashion! they wear great pads at the bottom of their backs — because pads are the fashion —

You then walk away 3 miles & look back again — you can just see the turretted stone Castle but not a glittering speck is visible! — and yet every little speck with corns, & indigestion, & toothake swears the Great Creator of all things, takes especial care of each of them, so that if they get relief from colic, they go down on their knees & thank him — if they go to War they ask his blessing, that they may cut more throats than their enemies & then if they do — they thank him again, with their bloody hands, for his great mercy!

These little specks are the most conceited little specks in Creation — they are so built, they must eat, & digest, if they eat too much, the blood goes to their brain, & then they see things quite different from what they are! — & then they doubt & disbelieve — if they do not — the Brain sees things *as* they are — & then they believe & are happy — so that sometimes they write long essays to prove there is no God, when it is only indigestion — & then long Essays to prove there *is* — & that is only *di*gestion so that *digestion* in reality is the cause of all the evil, & the Devil himself a personified bit of gristle, which can't get through the Colon, poor little specks, some cut their little throats, some take prussic acid — some hang themselves [1] — some say it is their fate when it is only their *conduct* — and all believe they'll go where there is no gristle, no indigestion, no blood in the head, no disbelief — or doubt of a God! — so these little specks die off & are succeeded by other specks.

The specks that die are buried, decay, become corruption, dress the ground, grow grass, feed cattle, & the specks which are the produce of the dead specks, eat often a bit of their own Parents, without being aware of it! & talk of the relish of the mutton! or beef — the taste of a ragout, or fricandeau! & then boast of the purity of their blood, their high descent, their birth, their honor!

After these lamentations, put St. Paul in your pocket — & you will return to Town with a true estimation of the value of Windsor Castle & its little specks.

Yours ever,<br>B. R. H.

*Address:* Miss B. Barrett / 50 Wimpole St.
*Postmark;* AU 16 1843

1. Haydon believed that Lord Castlereagh killed himself in 1822 because of indigestion caused by eating buttered toast (*Diary*, III,284; IV,316 and 319; and V,123).

# 88

*To Miss Barrett*
*August 29, 1843*

London Aug 29 1843

So you are evidently angry!—you did not like my disloyalty! —you know you did not—I shall send shortly for all my things with which I have encumbered you these 6 months. Books, oil & dissection of the Lion—

After all sorts of changes Alexander is settled in Composition—I have rubbed in Nelson signing the letter at Copenhagen in the height of the Fight—

Mary and my Daughter are in a Farm house at Southall, a sweet village, where the air is like champagne without the Sparkle—I get intoxicated with it—you can get to it in 10 minutes by Train—ls.3d.—What Times—

Did you see the precious document signed by Peel & Rogers & Lansdowne, their reason for giving Julius Caesar the Prize [1] —O Yes, O Yes, O Yes—this is to give notice—that all Committees or Commissions who wish to learn the Art of cutting their own throats with perfect certainty, may obtain advice (gratis) at the Royal Commission of *Fine* Arts from 10 till 12 Tuesdays excepted.

Signed

C. L. Eastlake, Secretary

God save the Queen!

How do you find yourself? not a word—you leave me alone in My glory.

Ever yours

B. R. Haydon

*Address:* Miss B. Barrett / 50 Wimpole St.
*Postmark:* AU 29 1843

1. See Letter 73, note 2.

# 89

---

*To Miss Barrett*
*August 29, 1843*


Tuesday Night Aug 29th 1843

I can't find any genteel paper so I tore half off a note of Sir
George Cockburn's who gave me a sitting today for a sketch;
as I sketch all extraordinaries I shall sketch you bye & bye—

Southall Green & Osterly are the (Norwood Green),[1] are the
very heart's core of pic-nics—We pic-nicked in a Corn field,
reapers & sheavers at work, & sucked in the air, till I was
tipsey—Is it not odd I can't work with half my energy now
Mary's face is gone—I do believe my boys love their Mother
better than any Girl they ever saw—they go on kissing her
so I am obliged to seize them by the collar & send them about
their business—Fred came ashore & rattled down on Sunday,
and after we had bid them good night—I missed the rascal
in the dark & he was gone back to have another kiss—Ought
I not to be jealous? I caught him & chased him away—I have
more wind than any of the dogs & can jump higher, & run
longer—I fear for Alexander. I am in an exquisite stretch
legging humour. I lie along, & hope to go on stretching like
Milton's death—A black cat came into the House last night.
That's *luck*, mind I predict it!—God bless you. When will you
roll up & see Alexander?

B. R. Haydon

*Address:* Miss B. Barrett / 50 Wimpole St.
*Postmark:* AU 30 1843

1. Southall Norwood is an urban district in Middlesex, twelve miles west
of St. Paul's Cathedral. Osterley Park is nearby.

## 90

*To Miss Barrett*
*August 30, 1843*

½ past five in the Morning
Aug 30 1843

And so you think I have not done my finest work!—I know it, my sweet Friend—the Crucifixion will be my last & greatest and then I shall mount—I could not sleep so up I got—

I have always prayed to see the Art reformed, & then I have always said I'll die, if it please my Creator—I have lived to see it reformed & to be its reformer but I am not dead & I humbly hope my merciful Creator means me yet for something more.

They have used me this year bitterly cruel to gratify the hatred of the Academy. Peel has no moral Courage—he did not dare make a stand, though he knew I deserved it—& Eastlake has less than his Master.

I was right opposite the Queen as she came from the Library in a front seat [of the] Painted Gallery, which I always choose in preference to the Body of the House where the Men are penned off like Cattle instead of being mixed with Women as we are in the gallery—if I am to be squeezed to death, allow me to say, the tender presence of a sweet darling, about or above me, I prefer, ten to one, to a brute who treads on your toes, & squeezes your ribs—I always feel inclined to strike out right & left—& clear a passage.

As she came I caught her large full Eye, right in my own, the most singular thing is I never see her jewels so powerful are her eyes—as she returned, I was looking sideways but I caught her looking directly at me, from the corner of my Eye, my glasses hinder any one seeing my look, I darted round my head in an instant, so quickly she couldn't escape, & I saw her large Eyes glance off, with an Effort, as Women do when they are caught—this is no vanity of mine—it is a fact—Upon my Soul it's truth—I assure you, & there was a momentary expression of *off her guard* in spite of her self possession.

Woman is Woman—Queen or not Queen—she seemed annoyed I had such evidence of being of sufficient consequence for *her* to look at—she couldn't escape, & her large eyes had that exquisite twinkle, when there is a little awkwardness, as there was, because she was annoyed.

I should think she was not a pleasant person, she has I'll bet my existence that detestable feeling of *not gratifying the Vanity of Man* & makes Albert feel it, I'll be bound,—Sad when I thought of *my* love, & looked at *her* (the Queen), what a Queen *she* would make, I'll send you a large study of her divine face tomorrow—I am going to see her in an hour, I don't think Cleopatra, or Aspasia, Thais, or Phryne, could beat her beauty—I am sure they couldn't—and so you'll think—

Your note last night was delightful, do not cease writing longer than a fortnight—I shall fine you two notes if you do.

Take care of my glorious Oil—& Believe me My dearest dream & invisible intellectuality.

B. R. Haydon

P.S. Be assured, my lecture did me immense good—I have recovered my self estimation, by such a defiance.

A black cat walked in to my house last night, jumped on my lap & purred—There's an end of Evil *this* Year—luck will now return—remember I predicted it.

# *91*

### *To Miss Barrett*
### *September 8 or 9, 1843*

London Sep 7th 1843 [1]

On my return from seeing my dear Boy on board the Giant Frigate Steamer of the World, 750 Horse power,—the Penelope, Tired – Sun burnt – breezy, hungry, & thirsty – I saw your hand writing. "Come," said I, "I will keep that 'with Wine of Attic Taste,'[2] and open it like a Walnut or a Filbert, and read it as I sip." Roll up! will you? – let me know, and I will receive you like a Poetess! – (I was going to write *Queen*) –

That assertion in the Times of my leading a party in the Pantheon, is an exquisite bit of Malice – I bespoke the Pantheon 2 months ago for myself[3] – in conjunction with no one – The Pantechnicon was offered which I declined. As I head no section, & join nobody in going to the Pantheon if Mr. East-lake can by his circular to the Papers, excite a rumour Haydon heads a Pantheon party & people go & find no body but Haydon the impression is, no body will follow Haydon, & Haydon's influence is injured! – Don't you see? – At first I contradicted it – Next year it will be said, "Nobody followed him to the Pantheon *you see!!!* " – Poor Haydon – The refinement is exquisite; they are all resolved to ruin my hold if they can – & By —— they shall not. I defy them! –

I agree with you my dear dream – in choosing Subjects – But who has painted the Crucifixion with the deep Religious feeling it ought to be painted with – no one. Am I to be he? – perhaps not – but I will try – I should no more think of painting the Dispute of the Sacrament, School of Athens, Heliodorus, Attila, Incendio de Borgo[4] – &c. &c. than of rewriting Macbeth – but when you come to "he bowed his head & gave up the Ghost"[5] I laugh to scorn[6] all Crucifixions ever done – There's presumption! Oh dear but it is genuine – I am engaged to lecture through the Winter – on Cartoons & Lord knows what –

I got leave for Fredric, & we lay on the grass in a spot Boccacio only *dreamt* of but *never saw* – It was the very place the Stories ought to have been told in the Decameron, if it be not *the* very spot – I maintain it is, & must be, I felt so inspired, I could have gone on with a second series!

Dear Boy! – Fredric – he is tall, handsome, & tender – he is going on Foreign Service – a dangerous service – I felt it – & so did he – he begged me not to go back with him – but

I did – and as I turned I saw him watching me with a spy glass – he waved his hat & so did I.

B. R. Haydon

There is nothing like danger! I could not live if I had not always the sensation of a precipice at my feet! – I glory in it! – Ah, My dearest Friend, how I would glory to die in a charge! – but I never shall! never! –

I relish not my Brothers in Art! – the poor uneducated unsword & pistol creatures! My boys are all capital shots – I made it a part of education, as much as Classics or morals! – Frank can hit a half crown – beware how they insult his Father's memory! After he beat 'em in Mathematics[7] – they took him out to rifle firing – thinking *here* we'll *do* him! – did they? I chuckled when I thought how his delicate & innocent face took them in – I am not a blood thirsty monster – Upon my word – but I had a great mind to enter as supernumerary today, when I saw the power of the Penelope – her Vast Wheels – her 68 pounders – the beams of her bow – sufficient to crash in a first rate – it will come to that – naval war will end in that – a Collision of prows like the Romans & Carthaginians – & then boarding.

Would you believe the family has not Nelson's sword, they don't know where it is!! These are descendants. It is the strongest argument for another World – where the Poetry if *this*, is the reality of *that*.

God bless you – we shall meet there.

*Address:* Miss B. Barrett / 50 Wimpole St.
*Postmark;* SP 9 1843

1. Evidence of the *Diary* and the postmark date this letter one or two days later than September 7. On September 8 Haydon wrote: "Went to see my Son Frederic on board the Penelope, who is going to Africa, I fear. We spent the day in a nook at Greenhithe worthy of Boccacio" (*Diary*, V,308). The letter is postmarked September 9.
2. Milton, Sonnet XVII, ll. 9–10. "What neat repast shall feast us, light and choice, / Of Attic taste, with wine."
3. The cartoon exhibition closed on September 2, and on September 4, Haydon moved his cartoons to the Pantheon (*Diary*, V,307–308).

4. Titles of frescoes by Raphael in the Stanze of the Vatican Museum.
5. John 19:30.
6. *Macbeth*, IV,i.79.
7. Frank Haydon obtained a first class in mathematics in 1843 at Jesus College, Cambridge.

# 92

---

## To Miss Barrett
## September 18, 1843

London Sep 18th 1843

My dearest Friend,

I send you Wordsworth, send me Wilkie—many thanks for your handsome present,—we have been eating Tamarinds ever since—the Polyphemi of Lemons we have not touched yet—

I am going to spend a whole day with a Lion & watch his savage & Royal Motions—how would I have gloried to have lived in such Times, when Lions were to be met with, taking an evening walk!

One of my day dreams used to be meeting a Lion in the Strand, escaped from Pidcock's[1]—& having a regular fight, when of course I laid [it] dead at my feet, & was carried on the Shoulders of the people—I have started up & huzzaed myself! before I got my perceptions—glorious!—Now I will realize a fight in my Picture—it is in a glorious state—do fix a day for a roll up—Best regards to your Sisters & family—

Ever yours

B. R. Haydon

P.S. Will you wait till the Lion's done, on reflection?—I'll give you a savage Monster, not the drawing room Lion, his Mane shining with Rowland's Calydor[2] like Edwin's for the Queen![3]

Did you ever see such an Egotist? I never ask you what *you* are doing, but take it for granted what *I* am doing must be delightful to you—

But what are *you* doing? because an Intellect like yours must be active.

*Address:* Miss B. Barrett / 50 Wimpole St.

1. Gilbert Pidcock's menagerie over Exeter 'Change in the Strand.
2. Rowland's Kalydor, "a creamy, odoriferous preparation from *Oriental Exotics,* is now universally known as the *only* safe and efficient *protector* and *beautifier* of the Skin and Complexion. Its virtues are commonly displayed in thoroughly eradicating all *pimples, spots, redness, tan, freckles,* and other unsightly *cutaneous defects,* in healing chilblains, chaps, and in rendering the most rough and uneven skin pleasantly soft and smooth. To the *complexion,* it imparts a juvenile roseate hue, and to the *neck, hand,* and *arm,* a delicacy and fairness unrivalled. To Gentlemen, it allays the irritation of the skin after shaving. Price 4*s.*6*d.* and 8*s.*6*d.* per bottle, duty included" (*The Athenaeum,* January 21, 1843, p. 71).
3. Haydon probably referred to one of Edwin Landseer's pictures of "Van Amburgh and his Animals," "the only pictures in which he can be said to have thoroughly failed; but the subject was unworthy" (W. Cosmo Monkhouse, *The Works of Sir Edwin Landseer,* London, [1879], I,89). The subject was unworthy because these were not wild but performing animals.

# 93

## *To Miss Barrett*
## *September 20, 1843*

London Sep 20th 1843

My dear Friend,

I spent the whole day with a Lion, & came home with a Contempt for the human Species!

Before we parted, we were Friends, & finding I was not disposed to torment him in any way he suffered me to pat his forehead, & smooth his paw—Perceiving I was worthy of his confidence, he stretched out & fell into a profound sleep, watching me now & then for the first half hour, but seeing I was no hypocrite, he fairly put his grand head back with the "abandon" of luxurious indulgence & roared & growled into forgetfulness—Before I went the Lioness was admitted and immediately assailed him with all the blandishments of attachment—Tickling herself with his grand mane, crouching beneath his grand paws & tumbling head over heels to attact his admiration![1]—'Twas delightful! The time came for *her* Majesty to retire but *his* Majesty blocked up the door & refused permission—The Keeper dropped the door on his nose, which started him back, & he was shut out instead of her—I then went round, & had him to myself in a sort of back court for 3 hours—& made some glorious studies—(Of course he was caged)—I hope to have a glorious Animal for you when you *do* come—

I came home knocked up—the heat of Sun shining into a sort of hot house at Cross (Surrey Zoological)[2] broiled one, the screeching of Macaws, the waspish snarls of leopards & Tigers, & eternal noises of birds & beasts from all the quarters of Earth, excited & distracted—

I came home outside an Omnibus & the Coachman dropped all my studies into the road, as a proof of his taste & grace in handing them to me—I dipped my face, head & neck in delicious cold Water—& putting myself in order for dinner spent the Evening after, looking over my studies & disputing with Frank & Hyman on the superiority of Milton to Byron in the Conception of Satan. How delightful it is to live to see Boys you first taught, come home distinguished & able to argue with their Father, who is able to argue with them.

I assure you, as Dunning said to Reynolds, when *we* meet the rest of the World is quiet at least—all eager, fierce & well read in both authors,—no one sparing the other—and maintaining our respective positions like Heroes—Good night &

Ever yours,

B. R. Haydon

1. Delicacy prevented Haydon from informing Miss Barrett that the lioness "was in heat, & as playful as a Kitten" (*Diary*, V,315).

2. "Surrey Zoological Gardens, Panton Place, Kennington, contained the menagerie of Mr. Cross, by whom the grounds were laid out in 1830–1832 after the demolition of Exeter 'Change. . . . The collection of animals was a very good one, the lions and tigers having been especially noted" (Henry B. Wheatley, *London Past and Present*, London, J. Murray, 1891, III,338).

# *94*

## *To Miss Barrett*
## *September 22, 1843*

London Sep 22 1843

My dearest Friend,

Will you return the Lion, as I want his Majesty — the Vol. of Wilkie you shall have — I have succeeded in the Lion's head I think giving in, & exhausted — My Lion is large & enormous in fact though the one I sent you is small.

Yours affectionately
B. R. Haydon

[*Haydon then drew a sketch of a long-eared dog, possibly Flush, though the legs are too long for a cocker spaniel. Flush had recently been returned to Miss Barrett after having been stolen.*]

*Address:* Miss B. Barrett / 50 Wimpole St.

# 95

To Miss Barrett
September 25, 1843

London Sep 25 1843

My dearest Friend,
   I beg you (if any pleasure to you) to keep my Portfolios till
I send for them —

Yours truly
B. R. Haydon

   I have been hard at work & am sallying [forth] for air — &
relief.

*Address:* Miss B. Barrett / 50 Wimpole St.

# 96

To Miss Barrett
October 6, 1843

London Oct 6 1843

My dear Friend,
   I hope on the whole you are pleased with our worthy The
Examiner yesterday.[1]
   Your defence of the Poetry of Harriett Martineau is worthy
of *her* — perhaps I could defend the converse — viz. there is
nothing Poetical but what is Radical — I could say just as
much on one side as the other. What I have a horror of is
the Ultimate republican vulgarity to which we are tending —
What is high art become? A beastly vulgarity already — the
solitary heroism, the mysterious sublimity, the awful singleness is gone! — every body now is profaning — I can no longer

stride my room by midnight & glory in feeling *alone* in my pursuit, from its dangers, its risks, its isolation! The Treasury with its vulgar thousands, have destroyed the danger, & therefore the honor. Upon the whole, I sympathise with the irresponsibility of a despotism, rather than the legal submission to law which characterises a Republic—this is my bond of sympathy with Napoleon & Alexander in preference to that namby pamby bit of moral worth Washington. In fact I am a contradiction my dear Friend, & to you alone I confess.

I gave Dennys[2] your note which sent him to the 3rd Heavens! His Portrait is my best—It was done in one sitting. If Tennyson has such a head, will you tell him I shall glory in painting him?[3] Uriel is getting on—& Satan settled—I make him springing off, maliciously glorying—& pointing to the Earth.

B. R. Haydon

1. *The Examiner* was published on Saturdays. The issue of September 30, which immediately preceded Haydon's letter, contains an essay "To Cornelius at Munich" (p. 611), deploring the fact that the names of most of the artists exhibiting in the cartoon competition were unknown outside of England.
2. Edward N. Dennys, a cotton-printer of Addison Terrace, who purchased Haydon's twelfth picture of "Napoleon Musing at St. Helena" and his second of "Uriel Revealing himself to Satan."
3. No portrait of Tennyson was painted by Haydon.

# 97

*To Haydon*
*October 7, 1843*

Oct. 7th. 1843

Oh my dear Mr. Haydon what are you thinking of me? That I am ungrateful beyond the "uses of this world,"[1] & that *that's* the best of me? And yet I have been very sensible to your kindnesses, & to the spirited excellencies of the last two chalk drawings which you sent me. Your chalk drawings always appear to me happy in power & expression — & these have the force of colour — & the orator's eyes quite flash through his spectacles from the extraordinary effectiveness of a few rapid strokes. Thank you (at last) for your goodness in permitting me to look at them — and if I did not say so at first, the reason does not dishonor my capacity of thankfulness, for I have had much to write — & writing much tires me. I can't "bite iron in two" as Mr. Haydon can: but he must use his power after the manner of his lion, — & spare. And besides I wrote last — Only it was of course my bounden duty to acknowledge the chalk drawings.

Have you a sketch of Macaulay? Did you ever see him?[2] A friend of mine is engaged upon a sequency to Hazlitt's "Spirits of the Age," & wants Macaulay's head for an illustration,[3] Macaulay the great Balladmonger I mean. You admire him I hope. You ought to do so, because he is a genius militant, after your kind — with a strong metallic ring in him; & an active beat, & resonance of voice. If you were to paint his Poetry, you would have to be pedantic in your anatomy, & bring out learnedly every possible sinew. No man can write a battle like Macaulay. If your Duke, who can fight one pretty well, were to try the writing of one, how cold & tame & cowardly it would seem in comparison to Macaulay's! Such is a poet's power! — to do everything *better* than the man who does it *best!*

I shall like to hear how your Alexander prospers — and whether you shall have a great work for the Exhibition which is coming.

Did I tell you that I had lost my little dog, & recovered him after three days, by a deep bribery of the dog stealers?[4] — Do you know what it is, to love a dog and lose him — & is it in your philosophy to pardon a tear shed by woman in such a cause? I, for my part, cried away all my character for sense, — but I recovered my dog & didn't care much. He threw himself into my arms in a mute ecstasy when he saw me again, with a full apparent consciousness of the wrongs & sorrows he had endured.

How is your daughter?

Ever faithfully yours
Elizabeth B. Barrett

*Address:* B R Haydon Esq. / 14 Burwood Place / Connaught Terrace
*Postmark:* OC 7 1843

1. *Hamlet,* I,ii,134.
2. Thomas Babington Macaulay (1800–1859) sat to Haydon on July 19 and August 24, 1833, to be included in the great picture of the banquet celebrating passage of the Reform Bill.
3. Richard Henry Horne's *A New Spirit of the Age* (London, 1844) contains a biographical sketch of Macaulay but no portrait.
4. See Letter 5, note 1.

# *98*

## *To Miss Barrett*
## *October 31, 1843*

London Oct. 31. 1843

My dear Miss Barrett,

I hope you have not been ill. Will you send me the Paradise regained – & Lucretia Mott – & Garrison (drawings) [1] –

Alexander himself is nearly done. Any Sunday from two till four I should be most happy to see your Sisters & Brothers or any Friends.

Yours most truly
B. R. Haydon

*Address:* Miss B. Barrett / 50 Wimpole St.

1. The American abolitionists Mrs. Lucretia Coffin Mott (1793–1880) and William Lloyd Garrison (1805–1879) attended an international convention in London in 1840. Haydon made portrait sketches of them and the other delegates in preparation for his "Anti-Slavery Convention," now in the National Portrait Gallery.

---

London Nov 4 1843

My dear Invisible,

The sight of thy Poetic, delicate, mysterious hand writing
was a comfort — I thought you had got tired or perhaps angry,
because I did not follow your advice! but I find *I* was silent
& not you, & so accept the Amende —

You asked me if I had known attachment to Dogs? — indeed
have I, before I had children, since, never. I had once a
thorough bred Newfoundland Pup, who got the Distemper &
when he was lying blind, & moaning near Death — on hearing
my Voice rose from his bed, staggered over on his trembling
legs, swinging to & fro from weakness, licked my feet, guided
by my Voice, trembling, staggered back, & Died wagging his
tail, & moaning affection — When my sweet Fanny an infant
was dying[1] — I said, "Fanny my love, d'ye love Papa?" Con-
vulsed as she was she stared towards me & died, smiling
devotion! So far, there was not much difference in feeling,
for my Sweet Fanny had hardly reason, so young. Perhaps
the Animal had as much so far — the difference would have
been in maturity.

I was so affected I did not recover it — I afterwards kept Grey
hounds Dr. Mitford gave me but they are callous brutes —
graceful & heartless.[2]

I supped out last night,[3] a meal I hate, with Artists & brutes
connected with Punch! What a scene! — a youth with a beard
told me, my defence of the English School & attack on the
German last year,[4] was translated into German at Vienna &
made a great noise at Munich — it did good he said, & put them
on the defensive about *line*, & mediaevalism.

Rumohr,[5] the first of critics, is dead — I corresponded for the
last year of his life — and his letters are invaluable.

As I have more Vanity than Pride, they say—I was pleased you liked the Sketch—it is interesting to me—poor Wilkie—how intimate we were then!—We got a party on the 10th & opened the great Barrow by the Church on the Hill, under the direction of poor Douglas, Author of Nenia Brittannica, a living Vicar of Wakefield—& we found as he said an Ancient British Urn, with the burnt bones of a Chief, the most Ancient mode of Burial—on the Rose ground we opened graves, & found skeletons Lying east & west, after Christianity. Douglas was a perfect Original & never surpassed.[6]

His theory was Urn burial on hills was before *Iron*—I said, "here's *Iron*"—"O God, I hope not," said he, & in he jumped & to his delight, found it *brass*—People of Fashion crowded about me, & began to steal relics!—Douglas jumped into the grave, & with his hat off, & his grey hairs moving to the sea breeze held forth on the wickedness of *disturbing the Ashes* of the Dead, *after* he had ascertained there was no *Iron*—& had tumbled about the Ashes in style! Never shall I forget the scene—

He invited us to breakfast (at Preston where he was Vicar), with Prince Hoare; I knew the man & breakfasted before I went & made Wilkie do the same—When we all three *met*—Douglas was *not up*—Breakfast was not laid—no fire in the Kitchen—Poor Hoare looked faint & gastly—at last we heard a flump out of bed, & suddenly Douglas called out—"Betty, where is my other stocking?"—which put Wilkie in such laughter, Hoare forgot his troubles—after 1 hour & $\frac{1}{2}$—We got a good Breakfast & a learned discourse—Douglas was the granary for all Colt Hoare's Book.[7] What are you going to bring out?

Yours ever & ever<br>
B. R. Haydon

*Address:* Miss B. Barrett / 50 Wimpole St.
*Postmark:* NO 4 1843

1. Fanny Haydon died on November 18, 1831, aged two years and eight months.
2. See Letter 24.

3. Haydon's diary for November 3, 1843, records his dining with William Kidd, a Scottish artist, Joseph Kenny Meadows, a draftsman and illustrator of Shakespeare, and several other artists, "one from Munich."

4. Haydon referred to his articles in *The Spectator* of November 12 and December 3, 1842.

5. Karl Friedrich von Rumohr (1785–1843), antiquarian, poet, traveler, art collector, and author of *Italienische Forschungen*, 3 vols., Berlin and Stettin, 1827–1831.

6. Haydon referred to archeological diggings which he and Wilkie made near Brighton in October 1815, under the direction of the Reverend James Douglas, whose book *Nenia Britannica* (London, 1793) is subtitled *A Sepulchral History of Great Britain (Diary,* I,477–478, and *Autobiography,* I,220 -222).

7. In his "Vita," an unpublished first draft of his *Autobiography,* Haydon wrote that Douglas was "the secret source from which Sir Richard Colt Hoare obtained all his information." Hoare (1758–1838) was a traveler and antiquary, author of *Ancient History of North and South Wiltshire,* 2 vols., London, 1812–1821.

# *100*

---

## *To Miss Barrett*
## *November 9, 1843*

London Nov 9th 1843

Now for Mesmerism! I am always inclined to believe in the wonderful, & do believe in the Supernatural, and therefore you may imagine, I went to ascertain the fact of Mesmerism inclined to be enthusiastic.

The Apostle Elliotson,[1] who in addition to his talents, has a fortune (a strong argument in favor of any scheme he starts) invited me to witness a remarkable case[2] – I went to his House by appointment, and with 4 or 5 others at Dusk sallied forth to Great Pulteney St I think. We entered a Parlor, where we sat some little Time, when a plain Sister came to us & told [us] *her* Sister would be there directly – In a few Minutes, a rather interesting compact, bending figure of a Girl followed, with something of an air of twisting & turning as she spoke, & half blushing & half giggling as she looked, not full at ye, but half sideways, between her curls which hung about her cheeks not altogether unbewitchingly.

A very fair subject thought I for a lark—Down she sat—& Elliotson began—very shortly her Eyes & lids drooped & closed, to a fixed sort of Closeness—Elliotson spoke as she was closing up, & she answered, till at last he said—"She is *gone*" & "now she is *rigid*." Every body took her hands—& they jerked to her body like Whale bone—Elliotson then sat on the Sofa with her, & called our attention to her sympathy—as *he* moved *she* moved, if he sat on her right—she gradually turned her head to the right, as if enamoured—if he went to the left so turned her head—if [he] laid himself on the ground, her head bent forward to the ground, in fact wherever he moved, she inclined herself.

He said this rigidity continues for hours—he stood up, so did she & whilst all were engaged in front of her examining her eye lids with a candle, I thought her arms looked *unrigid* —so slipping my hands behind her whilst I kept her attention by talking in front I caught her hand suddenly, *it was as loose as my own!* but the *instant* she *felt* a *touch—she stiffened it!* This *I will swear to*—from that moment I considered it a piece of imposture. I asked Elliotson about it, & told him with great delicacy the fact—he said *I must be mistaken!* I bowed & said nothing—but if all cases of Mesmerism are like this one— then the whole [thing is] falsehood.

I *defy* all Mesmerisers—I have travelled in the Coupée of the Mail to Liverpool with one—he & I alone—he said "I can mesmerise"—"can you" said I. "I defy you"—He began, I stared at him, fiercely, & after 10 minutes I burst out laughing, & he said "*I can't do it today.*" [3]

He was going to America by Steamer—I met him next day in the Streets, so putting my hand on his Shoulder I said, "Remember my Friend when at New York *You* did not put me to *sleep*"—at which he was exceedingly angry—Good Night—how odd—*I* thought *you* were tired of *me*. These people often separate.

B. R. Haydon

*Address:* Miss B. Barrett / 50 Wimpole Street
*Postmark:* NO 10 1843

1. John Elliotson (1791–1868), physician. In 1838 he was forced to resign his professorship of clinical medicine in London University because of his interest in mesmerism. In 1849 he established a "mesmeric hospital," and later he founded *Zoist*, a journal concerned with mesmeric healing.

2. The séance occurred on August 10, 1842, and is described in Haydon's diary for that date (V,192).

3. "October 19, [1838.] Left Town in the train, arrived at Liverpool . . . A young American sat with me in the Coupée, and heartily amused I was . . . He said he could animal magnetise. I defied him. He began with all his anticks, but I looked him sternly in the Face, & shook him. He pretended he was *ill*, and finding me awake broad, he said, 'Mayhap you are a *strong mind.*' 'So they say,' said I" (*Diary*, IV,527).

# *101*

---

## *To Miss Barrett*
## *November 9, 1843*

London Nov 9th 1843

Dearest Invisible,

I send you for a poetical feast, tonight before you retire, the very first proof (and you shall have the very first that is *published* from me) it is beautifully like — the very head —

Lupton[1] is my Man — let me have the large Canvas & keep this — till tomorrow 4 — pray take care of dust — as I must retouch — Your Eyes are the very first after the Painter & Engraver — there's an honor — *Bay* is nothing to it.

> Yours
>
> B. R. Haydon

My boy passed Examination for Mid — with Credit & is now a step higher, a regular middy.

*Address:* Miss B. Barrett / 50 Wimpole St.

1. Thomas Goff Lupton (1791–1873). Haydon's diary shows that he made engravings of "Wellington Musing on the Field of Waterloo" in 1840 and "Wordsworth on Helvellyn" in 1846, but it sheds no light on the engraving mentioned in this letter.

# 102

---

Novr. 10, 1843

I thank you cordially, my dear Mr. Haydon, for permitting me to take a glance at the exquisite engraving in its present state. It is beautiful indeed – the likeness striking; & the full expression of the picture admirably preserved. Believe me that I am sensible; yes, *sensitive* to the "priviledge" – & that my regrets on losing the great canvas, were softened by my sense of the kindness of it. As to your half expressed intention, I cannot suffer you to be so much *too kind* as to fulfill it really, because you know there is no reason why I should not make a purchase as well as the rest of the public. Let that pass – with my gratitude – that it should have occurred to your thought. You are very kind.

For mesmerism, my head aches so today that I am fitter to be a patient than a philosopher – but you will admit, I am sure, at once, that the existence of ever so much collateral deception is no argument against an essential truth. Perhaps you remember Coleridge's remark upon this very subject – "With every possible allowance for illusion, delusion, & collusion, there is yet a residuum for which I cannot account" – and I have heard within these few days "facts" as they are represented to be, upon evidence as rigid as your patient's arm was *not*.

There is a gentleman, known to a friend of mine, of an idiosyncrasy rather philosophical & historical, than poetical & fanciful – a "useful knowledge" man, by education a unitarian, – & by habit & temperament, carrying everything, through scepticism & investigation into inference – a man who will believe nothing, in fact, until it is proved – a logician in every act of his life, a grinder down of sentiments into ratiocinations. This gentleman set about investigating animal magnetism a few months ago — as he would investigate a problem — or a science. His *leanings* were, of course from his character, all *against* it — but upon a patient investigation he resolved. Of the facts which crowded on him, he threw many aside as fallacious, deceptive, or depending rather upon peculiar organization than peculiar power — and from these he patiently separated as "the residuum," other facts of evidence less exceptionable. By degrees he exercised the magnetic power himself, with various degrees of success. I think it was last week that he called upon his friend & mine, & said after some conversation —

"I wish to communicate to you some facts. I mention them to you as facts because they are parts of my experience: but I do not expect you, I do not ask you, I do not *wish* you, to believe them; as they are totally foreign to yours. This happened to me three days ago. Some friends were to assemble at my house to see me magnetize a subject. Before they came I went into my own room & locked the door, pushed back my sleeve, & with a penknife, cut a cross upon my arm; drawing the blood from the figure, I covered up my arm; mentioned it to nobody — went down stairs to receive my guests — & induced the magnetic sleep upon the subject.

"I said to her — 'I have a slight inconvenience at this moment. Can you tell me what it is?' She answered — 'I see your arm. You have cut it with a pen knife. I see the figure of a cross on it, yet wet with blood.'

"I continued my questioning. 'I have a house in Bath. Will you tell me something about it?' 'I see your house in Bath. There are rails before the door. It is surrounded by other houses with trees scattered between — and beyond, there is an extent of country which appears to me very beautiful.'

" 'Will you tell me now about the interior of my house?'

" 'I see a drawing room' — she described it minutely. 'I see such & such pictures' — describing them correctly in detail. 'And I see besides at the table a lady in black talking to another lady in white. Yes, I think she is in white – I do not see distinctly, but if not white, it is some very light colour – I think it is white.'

"'I have a son. Now tell me of my son.'

"'I see your son. He is a boy. He is writing at a table – and a lady leans over while he writes.'"

Continued the gentleman – "One of my friends went instantly to my house near London; and ascertained that my boy's writing lesson, which usually took place at eleven, had been accidentally delayed to twelve, the hour of the magnetic sleep, & that *at that precise hour* he was writing, while the lady who was his instructress leant over him giving directions. Moreover I went down myself to Bath, and called upon the lady to whom I had let my house. She was in deep mourning. I told her I had reasons for desiring to know her occupation at such an hour of such a day – and she replied that a female friend (dressed as she afterwards described in white) was paying her a visit at that hour of that day.

"Now," concluded the gentleman, "this is my precise experience of three days ago. I believe I am not *mad* – you would not call me *mad* upon ordinary subjects – & yet I come to you with this as my experience. Judge. I do not say – believe."

For my own part, my dear Mr. Haydon, I am thunderstruck – not believing, but thunderstruck. The strength of the evidence consists for me in the character of the *experiment*.

Think of a "useful knowledge" hard-headed man recounting these fairy tales as his *experience!* –

"And think of *you*," you will retort, "repeating this stuff to *me*, as if it were any other than fairy tales! I believe in nothing except – the pain in your head – & that must be so very dangerously bad, that I commend you into cataplasms."

Ever faithfully yours,
Elizabeth B. Barrett

My congratulations on your pleasure in your son – again & again.

# *103*

## *To Miss Barrett*
## *November 27, 1843*

London Nov 27 1843

I have finished Wordsworth,[1] you invisible Genius, you shall see it before it goes to the Engraver, & I hope you will say it is worthy of my Sonnet – How d'ye like "very like Papa about the Nose"?[2]

Yours affectionately
B. R. Haydon

Will you order your Servant to deliver my Jars of oil,[3] (left behind) to my man, when I send him?

*Address:* Miss B. Barrett / 50 Wimpole St.

1. "William Wordsworth," now at Dove Cottage, Grasmere, was painted between November 10 and 22, 1843.
2. The formal title of this picture is "The First Child." Haydon painted two versions of it, beginning the second on May 4, 1843.
3. See Letter 71.

# *104*

## *To Miss Barrett*
## *November 29, 1843*

London Nov 29 1843

Oh you couple of Conspirators! I'll be revenged, I'll go to Reading & walk about for 4 hours – & come back & *turn up my head* at 3 Mile Cross![1] see if I do not –

The Picture was painted to pay off a heavy medical bill – the Doctor, a Friend – & they are all Portraits – of the whole family — professionally employed — The Accouchée is the wife of the Son — who is amazingly proud of his Glory &c. Will you send by bearer the drawings of my Sleeping boy, indeed any framed drawings you may have, except *myself.* I am too proud to remain with you.

Fred was on Watch,[2] in that heavy gale, a Sea beat in the Cabin Windows & floated the Captain & knocked chairs & tables to atoms — he is a fine fellow, he talks of it as I would. I sympathise with the roar of Elements & seem to be in mine.

I have got through Alexander but have yet to revise — I rubbed in a Napoleon full size with such fury Monday I strained the ligaments of my right hand, & painted a small one[3] yesterday in $4\frac{1}{2}$ hours — bet on me! — Good God, when I look back on the last 9 months — & remember from what ruin I have been saved, never having yet received a single shilling for all last Year's labor, how gloriously I have kept my own position & the position of my dear Boys — & Women, can I feel otherwise than grateful to him who is invisible[4] and in whom I always trust with a daily intensity that is become a passion!

I met with a gem of a Napoleon standing in one of his attitudes, a cast — its price is only 6/ — shall I order it to be sent to you? I painted him musing at St. Helena. I'll paint him musing at *Erfurt, Kings* in his rear[5] — ha! ha! *Mum* — Was there ever such a Composition of Aristocrat, democrat, John Bull & Genius? — as the Immortal who signs

B. R. Haydon

*Address:* Miss B. Barrett / 50 Wimpole St.
*Postmark:* NO 29 1843

1. Miss Mitford's residence.
2. On H.M.S. *Penelope.*
3. These were Haydon's seventh and eighth versions of "Napoleon Musing at St. Helena."
4. Hebrews 11:27. "For he endured, as seeing him who is invisible."
5. This picture was never painted.

# 105

## To Miss Barrett
### November 30, 1843

London Nov 30 1843

My dearest Friend,

Will you send my drawings? by bearer—I hope you are well
—the little Queeny admired my Napoleon at Sir Bobby's [1]—
there's taste—but there it will end—

Yours always
B. R. Haydon

*Address:* Miss B. Barrett / 50 Wimpole St.

1. Sir Robert Peel purchased the first version of Haydon's "Napoleon
Musing at St. Helena," painted in 1830 and 1831, and hung it in his country
estate, Drayton Manor.


# 106

## To Miss Barrett
### about December 1, 1843

Dearest Dream,

Will you send my Studies of the Lion—& all my books. The
oil & Studies another Time—

Yours &c
B. R. Haydon

*Address:* Miss B. Barrett / 50 Wimpole St.

# 107

London Dec 19 1843

A merry Xmas to you, my sweet invisible — I awoke this Morning with a deep feeling of gratitude to God for the mere sensation of being alive & thinking — & I said

> Count o'er the joys thy days have seen
> Count o'er thy hours from anguish free
> And know whatever thou has been
> It's something better *still* to be.[1]

*Not* to be was Byron's — *Still* to be is mine & I maintain it is a healthier & nobler feeling —

You have been hard at Work & so have I — The Queen's Smile on my Napoleon brought orders for small repetitions at a small price, but I prefer painting cheap if I can keep out of debt — I painted 3 in 16½ hours and am painting a small Napoleon & Curtius, which you shall see before they go home because I think they will please.

By the bye I have sent you my Portrait — Can't you let me see yours? I think that's fair & like *Royal Persons!* Are we not Royal?

I move Alexander[2] in a day or two — to a larger Room for toning — Success to it — The Duke of Sutherland[3] called & thought it was too serious a business to make Alexander *smile* in Triumph — but I said No — The Lion was sinking — & Alexander would smile, at such a Victory. The Duke's exceeding mild & beautiful breeding shrunk at the Idea of fighting a Lion. I told his Grace I would give the World to do such a thing before I died! — I need not tell [you] *he* smiled — as much as to say "monté." I can't help thinking I do wrong, I should not let a Duke see *I* glory in what *he* thinks a danger! But he is such a delightful Creature, is so good a Friend & the

Dutchess too, that I pour forth, without the least hesitation before them – Do you know I am attached to the Aristocracy, I believe them as good as any of the other Classes – I know them to be – and I should regret to see their Class, so useful a check on people and Crown, lowered or crippled – though I feel I am a humble portion of the Mighty Spirit rising in the World, yet one would not like to see such a Class extinguished – why should it be wished, as it is, *I know* – It is more from envy than principle – the noble way in which they relieved Miss Mitford has raised them in the Scale of my esteem & I hope in yours –

Now the Sky is clearing I must to *brush* – So adieu, sweet Friend.

Ever Thine My sweet Friend, In Water or Wine

B. R. Haydon

Mary is just come down looking like an angel as you'd say.

B. R. H.

Take care of my *Oil*.

*Address:* Miss B. Barrett / 50 Wimpole St.
*Postmark:* DE 19 1843

1. Byron, "Euthanasia," ll. 33–36.
Count o'er the joys thine hours have seen,
Count o'er thy days from anguish free,
And know, whatever thou hast been,
'Tis something better not to be.
2. Haydon referred to his "Alexander's Combat with the Lion," finished on December 30, 1843, and exhibited at the Pantheon.
3. The second Duke of Sutherland (1786–1861), who purchased Haydon's "Cassandra" and "The Spanish Nun" in 1834.

# 108

## To Miss Barrett
## January 21, 1844

Sunday Jan. 21st. 1844

Now Ma'am, do you suppose I'll be content with a *written* Portrait, strong & pictorial as it is — I give you 6 Months to recover, & see me, and if you don't then, I shall be justified in coming to your Door & reproaching you through the Key hole — & that I'll do. You do not know, how delightful your words "My Son, thou art Invincible" sound yet in my *heart* not Ears — for it never went through them —

I have got Macbeth & George IV¹ all ready — I'll send you the Sketch of Macbeth to look at & cut up; *I* say it is a glorious conception — what will you say — I say Lady Macbeth is better in Sketch than in Nature. Mary says it is not — but she likes the feminine & graceful — I maintain — Murder must be guessed by her mien — Mary says she must still be beautiful & graceful — But *he is about it.* That which has made them *bold* has made me *drunk*² — 'tis no trifle.

What are you doing with your fine poetic soul, the highest poetry of Soul I know living. I have heard a capital sermon from Dean of Carlisle,³ on the Conversion of St. Paul, & the commemoration of that day next Thursday, I complete my 58th year & enter my 59th. I shall soon write 60! I only hope to cut out Titian in completing my 100th & then I'll die happy. I shall cut him out in nothing else — Think of the old Hero, dying of the plague prematurely cut off in his prime in his 99th year! ha-ha — could I but feel as I do now for 42 years longer how happy I should be — Is it nothing to have a strong clear brain, a vigorous body — activity, health, thought, gratitude to God; to have something to fight about, & fight for, to love & adore old England — & know I have advanced her Taste? — to be sure it is — I wake with aspirations of piety for feeling *alive.* I always did in Prison!⁴ — What an Unfortunate Man you are Haydon, said another last Year — Unfortunate? How — have I not my faculties & health, the Unconquerable Will! — & a beautiful face to look at — no, no, that is not Unfortunate — and have I not *female poets* who esteem & Inspire me? — I have —

B. R. Haydon

*Address:* Miss B. Barrett / 50 Wimpole St.
*Postmark:* JA 22 1844

1. "George IV and Wellington Visiting Waterloo." The visit occurred in 1821. Wellington wrote: "His Majesty took it very coolly, indeed never asked me a single question, nor said one word, till I showed him where Lord Anglesey's leg was buried, and then he burst into tears" (Philip Guedalla, *The Duke*, Hodder and Stoughton, London, 1931, p. 330).
2. Macbeth, II,ii,1. "That which hath made them drunk hath made me bold."
3. Very Reverend Robert Hodgson.
4. Haydon was imprisoned for debt in 1823, 1827, 1830, and 1836.

# *109*

## *To Miss Barrett*
## *February 6, 1844*

London Feb. 6 1844

My Dearest Friend,

I regret to give you bad news, but be assured there is a hidden power at work to lower me in public estimation, by the time the Houses are decorated, so that they may be able to step over & leave me out.

By manoeuvre & intrigue Alexander could not be hung up. Two old Pictures, Saragossa & Napoleon were selected which the public have seen, & Alexander which they have not seen is turned out — I have instantly moved it to the Pantheon, & I beg your family to go & see it & do me justice.

I attribute it to the following cause —

The Duke of Sutherland gave me leave to finish it, at the British Gallery before it opened. The Keeper, a Mean spitish person was out of Town, I wrote him, & moved in, but I found he was annoyed because I *did not* wait!

I sent Napoleon & Alexander but *he* advised me to send Saragossa — (3) — foolishly I did, and I have no doubt the opportunity of being so unconscionable as to send 3 gave my enemies in the Committee an excuse for preventing my following up the blow of Curtius by Alexander. Thus I have been 11 months & received no reward for my labors — & I dread the Consequences after all my struggles! — I fear to tell *all* my difficulties to Mary — for you may imagine how much I have managed to defer & arrange to get through such a work. First came the Cartoons, & now this Alexander affair, no effort I make seems to be rewarded — Do not imagine I fear for myself, I do for my dear Family, for the sale of it, I fear is ruined —

> I am Yours Anxiously
> B. R. Haydon

I assure you it is one of my finest things.

# *110*

---

*To Miss Barrett*
*February 8, 1844*

London Feb 8 1844

My Dearest Friend,
I am always willing to do any thing I am employed to do, I paint small or large, but I of course do that, when not employed, my Soul glories in.

In my ultimate success is involved a principle, viz. whether

Power when it oppresses is to be resisted or submitted to? That is the reason I hold out, & will to the last.

Instead of finding fault because the Patrons do not rise to my level, you all blame me for not descending to theirs – For my interest you are right, but what a shocking state of taste.

If I should request your protection of my box again I hope you will grant it.

I am now painting (small) George IV visiting Waterloo with the Duke and I have rubbed in Macbeth *after* the Murder; depend on my putting forth regularly small saleable things as well as large –

In the Pictorial Times of last Sunday & next Sunday he speaks of the Cartoon as (*I* think) it deserves.[1] He has penetrated into my meaning & thoughts & principles – do get 'em both –

Yours always

B. R. Haydon

*Address:* Miss B. Barrett / 50 Wimpole St.
*Postmark:* FE 12 1844

1. The *Pictorial Times* published four articles entitled "The Proposed Decorations of the New Houses of Parliament." With copious quotations from *Paradise Lost*, the author enthusiastically described Haydon's cartoon "The Curse" (more frequently known as "Adam and Eve") in the issues of Saturday, February 3, and Saturday, April 20, 1844 (pp. 68–70 and 248). The former article included an engraving of the cartoon, showing Adam, Eve, Christ, Satan, and the serpent. "What artist is there," the author wrote, "no matter his name or fame, who attempting to represent such character, has not utterly failed? To say that Mr. Haydon has, in this work, succeeded beyond all the rest, is our highest praise."

# 111

*To Miss Barrett
February 26, 1844*

London Feb 26 1844

It is true—my faces tend to a Standard, & may resemble, because I choose Heroes, & Gods, & they are of a Kidney—and therefore your Friend, whose opinion is not worth a straw, has with his straw tickled me to reflection.

We have been wretched, & Mary quite worn out with anxiety about my daughter—we feared her spine, & Elliotson has examined her & pronounced it straight as an arrow & perfect & no cause for alarm. She has nothing but weakness left—*nothing* but *weakness!* as if that was nothing—The necessity of examination has hurt her feelings & she has been crying ever since—dear little soul, her mother is worn out—it is hard work with the sick, if their temper gives in, but we who are well ought to remember their condition. I hope Spring & Summer will do the rest for her.

I have been painting small Napoleons—& a *set* of his Musings. 1 musing in his garden at Fontainebleau in *his glory!* 2 musing in his bedroom the night before his abdication. 3 musing over the King of Rome in his Cradle—4 musing at St. Helena! I feel the truth of his own saying as applied to himself "Je suis moi seul une revolution!" Now he gains as Posterity approaches.

Poor Hazlitt!—after Waterloo, he went about for a Month getting intoxicated at all the public houses from despair—& *then he relinquished drinking for Ever*—a fact—

I have prepared Macbeth on the Staircase, after the Murder, Lady Macbeth looking murder & listening—I send you the Sketch to look at, the Painting is large. I have sketched Christ looking down on the Temple in its Splendor, & foretelling its ruin—& *George IV & the Duke at Waterloo!* But these are straggling struggles—My Soul is longing for a

Fresco Dome like St. Paul's—"Ah the pity of it Iago—the pity of it."[1] I shall go out of the World like a Lion in an iron net, who did nothing but roar till he died. Like Lear on my death bed I shall say, "Stretch me no longer on the rack of this tough World."[2]

Jersey!—no—to drink vinegar claret, where the Sea is ever lukewarm, & people anomalous English & French!—If you knash your teeth, I'll bite my lip in two—She is dreaming—or idle—or capricious, or plaguing—if she go, I'll write her Epitaph—

Adieu, my dear Friend—I'll have *both* jars of oil if not troublesome—

Ever & Ever—Amen<br>B. R. Haydon

*Address:* Miss B. Barrett / 50 Wimpole St.
*Postmark:* FE 27 1844

1. *Othello*, IV,i,206–207.
2. *King Lear*, V,iii,314–315. Immediately before killing himself, Haydon inaccurately quoted these lines as the last words in his diary.

# *112*

---

## *To Miss Barrett*
## *March 8, 1844*

There is nothing in our Art mechanical—even what is called so—when perfectly done in its mere imitation. It is evidence in perception of the "ponere totum" *which* is evidence of grasp & power of comprehension the reverse of mechanical.

There is some truth in all you say of Macbeth—& it will have its effect—but did you ever know the Resaugusta [?] dome [?], if so, you will feel why I paint Napoleons at so much a head—I have painted 13 Napoleons musing at St. Helena,

6 other musings – & 3 Dukes & Copenhagens – the best is Napoleon at Sunrise musing on the Pyramids.

I am Lazy, fidgetty, discontented, & dull tonight. So God bless you & good night or I may have an Effect.

I am going to Liverpool to lecture & Manchester & then home for the Royal Institution. I go 20th.

If *our* Mitford *will go* let her – she'll soon complain & long for 3 mile Cross.

B. R. Haydon

*Address:* Miss B. Barrett / 50 Wimpole St.
*Postmark:* MR 8 1844

# *113*

---

### *To Miss Barrett*
### *April 9, 1844*

Liverpool April 9 1844

My dear Friend,

Gower was yours, I presented it to you.[1] I return it, pray honor it –

Do let me see the Sonnets. I have not heard from the Poet – lately –

I conclude Saturday after a most brilliant Course. You must know I was mainly instrumental in founding a School of Design here – & made the figure as at Lyons the basis – when I was gone my principle & the Lyons school principle, being in opposition to the Monopoly in London, was *abolished.* The Young Men were so convinced of the soundness of my views – they re-assembled privately – subscribed, & continued on the principle I had taught them – They have brought me their drawings – & they are capital. This is like the early

Christians – persecution is the root of successful reform – and all over the Country they are doing the same.

Is it not glorious? – I defy the Infernal Spirit of Monopoly whenever I meet its selfish Sneer! – I'll give it a tint of persecution & that will do more than all my preaching –

Have you seen Napoleon's opinion in Council? translated by Capt. B. Hall[2] – also Memoirs du Consulat![3] – capital, capital – how I enjoy Napoleon, what a singular composition of enormous Genius; paltry weakness; magnificent extension of view, & pettiness of principle, yet he kept his oath & never sacrificed a village of the Empire from Hamburgh to Paris, & he died like a Hero on a Rock, because he wouldn't "Decidunt Turres."[4] It is that noble singleness of moral firmness that endears his Memory to me – though I glory the Duke beat him –

                                        B. R. Haydon

Get *United Service* Journal of *February* & see B.R.H. defence of Waterloo[5] – Lord Fitzroy [Somerset] told me it was the strongest thing he had seen.

*Address:* Miss B. Barrett / 50 Wimpole St. / London
*Postmark:* Manchester AP 9 1844

1. Probably a sketch of Gower. Among the Haydon-Barrett correspondence is an empty wrapper addressed to Miss Barrett, postmarked FE 12 1844, and endorsed by Haydon on the lower left corner "Gower."
2. Captain Basil Hall, R.N., published his translation from the French of Baron Pelet de la Lazère, *Napoleon in Council, or the Opinions Delivered by Bonaparte*, Edinburgh, Robert Cadell, 1837.
3. Probably Count Antoine Claire Thibaudeau's *Mémoires sur le consulat, 1799 à 1804* (Paris, 1827).
4. Horace, *Odes*, II,x,11.
5. Haydon's letter, headed "Battle of Waterloo" and dated January 15, 1844, appeared in *Colburn's United Service Magazine* of February 1844 (44:279–281). He defended Wellington against detractors who argued that Waterloo was won by luck rather than by military genius.

# 114

## To Miss Barrett
## May 29, 1844

London May 29 1844

My dearest Friend,

How we have separated, no notes, enquiries, or interchange. I fear you are ill. I have been working hard, & lecturing & am now "On Satan in likeness of an Angel enquiring the way to the Earth of Uriel disturbed from Meditation."

Do let me hear of your Poem & of you

& Believe me

Still yours ever

B. R. Haydon

*Address:* Miss B. Barrett / 50 Wimpole St.
*Postmark:* MY 31 1844

# 115

## To Miss Barrett
## May 31, 1844

London May 31 1844

Mary Mitford is a Darling for not going to Cockney Jersey — with namby pamby wine, fresh Sea, & no East Winds to brace her.

I am painting Uriel & Satan [*a sketch of the subject*]. There's for ye! — you darling Poetess! — I am printing my lectures [1] — & have just read first proof. I'll be hanged if the Sketch other side is not finer than the Picture — and I shall

absolutely alter from it – if I want it for a morning – let me
have it – not unless I ask –

My sweetest Mary is well & my daughter moving towards
recovery –

Do let me see your 1st Vol.[2] – as soon as you can –

I am My dearest Friend
B. R. Haydon

No pain in Earth is or can be as severe as the raptures of
Genius on Abstraction are delightful. Is it not true?

1. *Lectures,* 1844. The dedication to Wordsworth is dated September
1844. Haydon published a second volume of *Lectures* in 1846.
2. *Poems,* 2 vols., London, Edward Moxon, 1844.

# *116*

---

*To Miss Barrett*
*August 31, 1844*

London Aug 31 1844

My dearest Friend,

I am going to ask you a great favor – My dear daughter is
still delicate & anxious to employ her mind. She wishes, & I
no longer oppose it, to educate a genteel child from 4 to 10 – in
English, French, Italian & Music. Is it in your power to plant
her in that point as Daily Governess?[1] – She's a gentle Creature, & will see you, if you can see her – & I shall be everlast-
ingly obliged, if you get her *something to do* –

Your faithful Friend
B. R. Haydon

*Address:* Miss B. Barrett / 50 Wimpole St.
*Postmark:* AU 31 1844

1. Writing to Miss Mitford on September 1, 1844, Miss Barrett summarized Mary Mordwinoff Haydon's hopes for employment. "Her father has written to beg me to do what I can to meet her wishes," she wrote; "*I*— what can I do? But *you*, who know everybody in the world, may know some evil disposed person in town, inclined to torture his or her poor child" (Miller, pp. 221–222).

# *117*

## *To Haydon* [1]
## *after October 5, 1844*

I had felt some apprehension from the thunders in that quarter. The delay had seemed to me ominous; and although a criticism will not kill a book which is not right mortal, and although we authors may say so over and over to ourselves, yet before such a critic as Mr. Forster, of the "Examiner," we must not affect an impossible indifference. He is the ablest of English critics, and for his kindness to my little volumes I am grateful.

Ever most faithfully yours,
Elizabeth Barrett

1. The location of this letter is unknown. Frederic Wordsworth Haydon (*Correspondence*, I,461) printed it immediately after a letter from Haydon to John Forster (1812–1876), who was assistant editor of *The Examiner* from 1834 to 1847, at which time he became editor. The letter from Haydon to Forster is erroneously dated October 9, 1845. Haydon wrote: "My seven first Lectures will be published on the 17th [of October 1844] . . . I trust you will honour me by one of your first-rate criticisms. I am delighted at your remarks on Miss Barrett, and so was she. Your criticisms really are treasures." *The Examiner* reviewed Miss Barrett's *Poems* on October 5, 1844.

# *118*

*To Haydon*[1]
*October 30, 1844*

October 30, 1844
50 Wimpole Street

It is your own fault, my dear Mr. Haydon, if I have not yet quite finished your work. You desired me to read a lecture a day and I have been as perfect as I could in my obedience. It is a very interesting work – & the very faults of it – or what appear to me to be such – add some thing to the interest, by giving an appearance of precipitate & uncalculating ardour on the part of the writer. The individuality also is marked in broad lines – we have not to deal with lectures on art by an artist, but with lectures by B. R. Haydon on *his* art, – and this of course I like. The anatomical parts appear to me to be too much detailed & not sufficiently developped, – I mean, that, without example, – more example than you give, – a pupil unacquainted with anatomy, might receive a heap of words in many places, & confused ideas in their connection. I tried it, at least, with myself, and on one or two points your plates appeared to me insufficient. But your argument in favour of the *necessity* of anatomical studies, I take to be a conclusive argument, – put with great vivacity but supported with no less logic.

Notwithstanding what I said of the good effect of some of the "very faults," I certainly wish that some of them were away – I wish that your language were more correct & specific than it is sometimes, and that several things had been omitted, which according to my impression, sin against good taste. Also I think you use some disrespectful expressions in speaking of Michael Angelo, – expressions contradictory to the admiration you in another place profess for him. And I do not agree in what you say of Shakespeare, – in the analogy you suggest between his use of an historical fact &

Raffael's use of Michael Angelo's success in Art. If you had said that Shakespeare triumphed with the language . . .

1. Mrs. Madeleine Buxton Holmes gave permission to publish this fragmentary letter and provided the transcript made by her father, M. Buxton Forman, Esq. The letter was sold at Sotheby's on June 27, 1972; Paul Grinke, Esq., purchased it.

# *119*

---

## *To Haydon*
## *November 14, 1844*

November 14 1844

Of course I shall like to see a leaf from a book of Reynolds's,[1] my dear Mr. Haydon—but I can only *conceive* of the interest attaching to the specific details you mention. Alas! I am too ignorant! As to Pindar & the Greek quotation, why should you mind? The printer mistook—and that is all. Nobody will think of it again.

The Critic should have gone to you before now—but it has been lent to somebody. You shall have it in time, & do not be uneasy; for, as far as my recollection extends, you were far better treated in it than I was.

I did not understand anything you said as a reproach. You are always very kind to me, & I am not apt to stand in a corner & listen for occult offences. Why, what *is* Flush, but a lapdog? And what am *I*, but a woman? I assure you we never take ourselves for anything greater—and *Flush* I would rather have *less*, considering how often he comes rolling over my head from the cushions behind, like an avalanche.

Ever most faithfully yours
E. B. Barrett

1. "Early in 1844 Haydon was in correspondence with Sir Joshua Reynolds's niece, Mrs. Gwatkin, who had in her possession many of his papers. Haydon proved, with her aid, that Burke had not 'touched up' Sir Joshua's Discourses" (Shackford, p. 74).

# *120*

London No 15th 1844

I enclose you the precious document – a leaf from the *real* Koran – I bring it myself for fear of Earth quakes – & will send for it to-morrow – Place it under lock & key. Take care of dear little Blush [*sic*].

Yours ever,

B. R. Haydon

I sent Mary Russell – the Lectures – [on] to day's train – with all the Greek right – I am horribly sorry for I shall lose the *little* Classical repute I had imposed on the World.

Miss B. Barrett

1. This letter is in the Wellesley College Library.

# *121*

London Dec 29 1844

Since I have been in Town 40 years – I never [saw] "such a darkness at noon-day." [2] It was a darkness that "might be felt." As I groped my way home from Vere St. Chapel, the Park was splendid, the Sun had spread out all over Kensington, whilst all over the Edgeware Road it was murky, the Effect as if Moscow was burning to the South! I never saw anything so Splendid!

In Church it was exquisite, a living Rembrandt – the Clergyman with his four candles was lighted up in a glory, whilst the mighty shadow of the sounding board e[n]velloped the Ceiling – the Windows were hardly visible, against the dingy Sky – & the Congregation so many sombre masses of dim obscurity – I shall make a Sketch [*a sketch of the church*]. There's a Sketch for you.

Aristides is all on the large Canvas. I send you the Sketch.

He is appealing to the Gods as he leaves the Piraeus – & hoping the Athenians may never again want the advice of Aristides.

His wife with her Infant – & his Eldest boy holding by Aristides – are the group. Themistocles on the left, enjoying the banishment of his Rival – the Acropolis & Parthenon (20 years before it was built) is behind the walls & Towers of Athens, &c. – mob hooting – this illustrates the injustice of Democracy. The next will be the horrors of Despotism.

Adieu, the Fog is coming.

Yours always & longer,<br>
B. R. Haydon

1. This letter is in the Wellesley College Library.
2. William Cowper, "The Progress of Error," ll. 448–451. "The Will made subject to a lawless force, / All is irregular, and out of course, / And Judgment drunk, and bribed to lose his way, / Winks hard, and talks of darkness at noonday."

# *122*

---

## *To Miss Barrett* [1]
## *February 13, 1845*

London Feby 13th 1845

I am almost afraid to ask how you are? If you are not ill will you spare me the Cupid & Psyche, my oil Sketch, and *lend* me your copy of your Poems—Frank has taken mine to Cambridge. I am Winging[?] Uriel.

Yours ever,<br>B. R. Haydon

Miss B. Barrett

1. This letter is in the Wellesley College Library.

# Appendix

An unpublished imaginative memoir by Haydon, strongly auto-biographical, entitled "A Tale of the Court of Magnificent 1st," concerns an artist called Ardour. It is found on four holograph pages following the entry in Haydon's diary for March 8, 1830, recording the fact that George IV failed to buy his "Punch, or May Day," a companion piece to "The Mock Election," purchased by the King in 1828. Haydon attributed his inability to sell the picture to the duplicity of his former friend, William Seguier, who appears in this memoir as Cunning, the connoisseur. David Wilkie, from whom George IV purchased twelve pictures, is characterized as the artist Caution.

## A Tale of the Court of Magnificent 1st

In a certain sea were two large islands, comprising three Kingdoms, over which reigned a Monarch so celebrated for his sagacity, his acquirements, his exquisite manners, his delightful conversation, his splendor of taste, and his magnificence of view, that his subjects who all loved him and his attendants who all adored him greeted him by the name of Magnificent 1st.

At his coronation, when he first issued from behind his Throne and gracefully fell, as it were, into his seat, his bow of recognition to his Foreign Ambassadors and beautiful Peeresses was by him who had seen it never to be forgotten. It was the bow of a human being taught from infancy for 60 years that all other human Creatures were below him. It was a bow that consoled them as it were for their destiny but confirmed them for ever in it. It was the condescending remembrance of a superior creature.[1]

Magnificent 1st was a great Patron of the Arts of the Country over which he ruled, and when he judged from his own native sound feeling, he seldom judged wrong.

When he came to his throne, his capital city was the largest & most tasteless in the World in Architectural ornament, but such was the energy [of] his will and the richness of his taste that in a few years those who had left it in youth & returned to it in manhood scarcely believed their eyes.

What had happened in Architecture had happened also in other Arts. Sculpture made great advances, and Painting absolutely all her former effects.

In the dominions of this magnificent Monarch were two Painters of distinguished talents, the one called *Ardour* and the other *Caution*, and in the immediate court of Magnificent 1st and about his person was a Connoiseur, who was so remarkably honorable in money transactions, so conscientious in what he recommended Magnificent 1st to purchase, that the most unqualified reliance was placed upon his discretion, his prudence, his honor, and his taste.

His name was *Cunning*. He was shrewd and sagacious, with a quick sense of the ridiculous. He knew mankind well and despised them heartily, he had great powers of mimicry, and not his most intimate Friends escaped. The Monarch himself and the nobility of his Court would occasionally be held up in confidential moments; he saw only in mankind what was not estimable; nobody loved him, and he loved nobody—he envied talent, hated superiority, and had such apprehension lest anyone should share the confidence of the Sovereign whose taste he guided that there was nothing mean, malicious, unjust or untrue that he would not be guilty

1. Having attended the coronation of George IV on July 19, 1821, Haydon drew upon his memories for this description (*Diary*, II,348–351).

of if he could check the advance to honor and to rank of those who deserved to be rewarded or keep the Monarch to himself.

*Ardour* was a painter of great talent, and so was *Caution*. Ardour was ambitious to honor his Country & his Sovereign — *Caution* thought only of himself, which Ardour seldom thought of. *Caution* secured his own comforts, while *Ardour* was always led by his imagination and rarely found the reality equal the idea. Caution never offended and seldom delighted, while Ardour delighted often and offended much. Nobody loved or hated Caution, while Ardour was hated by some as heartily as he was adored by others.

Magnificent the 1st had long patronized *Caution* — and Ardour having painted a Picture of a singular subject — Magnificent 1st sent for it and bought it. *Cunning* was the agent, but the evident mortification with which he executed the commission of his Sovereign shewed Ardour *at once* he was the unwilling instrument of the act.

Those about Court blamed *Cunning* for his simplicity in not framing excuses or causing delays, by which the Monarch might have been irritated with *Ardour* & sent his Picture back, or prohibited its coming after all. They said, "*Cunning*, you are a simpleton to do things in so straightford a manner," — and *Cunning* promised better behaviour in future.

It happened two years after this *Ardour* painted two more subjects, and Magnificent wishing to patronize *Ardour* ordered *Cunning* to be written to — to go & see the Pictures & if they were fine to bring them down. *Cunning* now said to himself, "I won't be blamed again for being a simpleton now," & so he went to Ardour and said he had been ordered to see the Pictures and, said *Cunning*, "if the King wishes to see them, how can it be managed?" "Oh," said Ardour, "the King shall have them directly." "But," said Cunning, "I must see the King first." Now *Cunning* had in his pocket the letter wherein the King had ordered *Cunning* to bring the Pictures down if they were fine. On the day this passed, the grandees of the Court were all coming to see the Pictures — and Ardour said, "if any nobleman wishes to buy the Picture which is for sale, what must I do?" "Oh," said *Cunning,* "sell it at once," thus entirely concealing from Ardour the wish of Magnificent the 1st and urging Ardour to sell Pictures which the King had expressly ordered Cunning to bring to him before any body else saw them – and as it were laying a trap for Ardour to fall into, by which he must have offended his Sovereign, and urging Ardour to sell what his Monarch wished first to see, & thereby Cunning hoped stopping all future communication from the King.

The next day *Cunning* saw the King – and the King of course thought his orders had been obeyed. But no – *Cunning* did not tell the King that *Ardour* was unacquainted with his wishes, but he said the Public would be disappointed if Ardour's Pictures were not first shewn, and the King being a perfect Gentleman, acquiesced directly, and ordered the Pictures down after the Public had seen them.

But Kings expect as they have a right their orders to be obeyed, and there is no doubt Magnificent 1st must & did think Ardour an illbred ungrateful man to resist the wishes of his Sovereign, not knowing, alas, that Cunning took care the wishes of his Sovereign should not be communicated till it was too late to execute them. Else in an instant would Ardour have flown to execute the orders of his generous Sovereign, a Sovereign who by the purchase of his other work had rescued *Ardour* from ruin – and who evidently wished to do so again but who had been thwarted in his noble wish by the base intrigue of the basest of his attendants, an attendant whose selfishness is only equaled by his cunning, and his cunning by his malignity.

Caution & Ardour began life together. When Caution came to one of those precipices which intersected the great road, Ardour was always for taking a run and clearing it by a leap, while Caution preferred descending by the foot path, crawling at the bottom & mounting safely on the other side. Ardour as might be expected sometimes broke his shins & sometimes his head & sometimes he leaped over all & stood huzzaing, but he often saw Caution steadily fagging away

while he was rubbing his skin in agony & Nelson[?] trick-
ling[?] out of his eyes. *Ardour's* great pleasure was danger,
while Caution's was safety. The consequence was that
Caution got into the Court of his Sovereign while Ardour
got into his Prison.

And there is no doubt that *Ardour* would always get into
his Sovereign's presence but Cunning & Caution being
before him, every body must allow if he succeed in baffling
Cunning and outwitting Caution he will be an extraordinary
fellow too. But alas Caution might be at last induced to see
no danger in letting *Ardour* in — but who can be a match for
Cunning, who can be a match for a creature who conceals
his Sovereign's wishes from *Ardour,* and misrepresents
Ardour's intentions to his Sovereign. [*The final sentence
is largely illegible.*]

# Index

Aaron, 134
Abrantes, Duchesse d', 56
Acre, 52
Adam, 13, 110
Aeschylus, 108; *Agamemnon,* 97,
109n.; *Prometheus Bound,* xi
Albert, Prince, 87, 113, 125n., 144
Alcibiades, 38, 39n.
Alexander the Great, 152, 166
Alexander I, Emperor of Russia, 72
Allan, Sir William, 95
Anglesey, first Marquis of, 169n.
*Annual Register, The,* 42n.
Antibes, 52n.
Apollo, 84
Apollonius, 33n.
Apsley House, 57n.
Ardor, Henry, 132, 133n., 185–189
Aristides, 182
Armitage, Edward, "Caesar's First
Invasion of Britain," 121, 122n.,
126, 141
Artaxerxes I, 57n.
*Art-Union, The,* 108, 109n.
Aspasia, 144
*Athenaeum, The,* xii, 4–6, 7n., 33,
34n., 36n., 37, 38n., 39, 70, 72n.,
80f., 84, 122n., 128n., 134n., 148n.
Athens, 182

Barnum, Phineas, xiv
Barrett, Arabel (E.B.B.'s sister), 3n.
Barrett, Edward (E.B.B.'s brother),
x, 19n., 26
Barrett, Edward Moulton (E.B.B.'s
father), x, xi, 18, 19n.
Barrett, Elizabeth Barrett
   —publications of: *Aurora
   Leigh,* xv; *The Battle of Mara-*

*thon,* xi; *Casa Guidi Windows,*
xv; Chaucer, translations from,
33, 34n.; "Crowned and Buried,"
xvii; "The Cry of the Human,"
37n.; "The Dead Pan," 37n.;
*Letters,* xx, 38n.; "The Lost
Bower," 37n.; "Napoleon's Return," 70, 72n.; *Poems,* xv,
177f.; *Prometheus Bound,* xi;
*The Seraphim,* xi, 5, 6n., 9n.;
"Sonnets from the Portuguese,"
ix; "Sonnet on Haydon's Picture
of Wordsworth," 4, 42, 43n.
   — alleged obscurity of poems of,
9, 11, 78; argues with B.R.H. on
Napoleon and Wellington, xvi,
50f., 54, 68–72, 78; argues with
B.R.H. on mesmerism, xvi, 157,
160–162; belief in spiritualism,
xvii; birth of, xi; B.R.H.'s hope
that she will edit his memoirs,
xv, 109; changes rooms, 93f.;
death of, xv; delicate health of,
ix–xi, 9, 11, 18f., 36f., 44, 47, 82,
94, 106, 117; defends H. Martineau, 151; describes self, 18f.;
elopement of, ix, xv; enjoys
B.R.H.'s memoirs, 20–24, 26,
27n., 81f., 105f.; gifts to B.R.H.,
147; gratitude at B.R.H.'s loan
of pictures, 2, 14, 17, 68, 156,
160; grief at B.R.H.'s death,
xiv, xv; interest in B.R.H.'s children, 69, 162; interest in Keats,
xvi; lends B.R.H. her Chaucer,
33; love of Flush, 153f., 180;
love of London, 36; meeting
with Wordsworth, 3, 4n.; opinion
of Lady Byron, 69; opinion on

evil, 13; politics of, xiii; punctuation of, xviii; reads B.R.H.'s *Lectures,* 179; receives letter from Wordsworth, 6, 7n.; receives B.R.H.'s tea urn, 7, 79, 82–84, 87–89, 91; refuses to permit B.R.H. to call, xvi; takes charge of B.R.H.'s papers, 118–120; use of drugs, xi; sympathizes with B.R.H.'s disappointments, 128
Barrett, Henrietta (E.B.B.'s sister), 3n.
Bath, 161f.
Bathurst, third Earl, 59, 61n.
Beaulieu, Jean Pierre de, 52
Beaumont, Sir George, xii, 24, 25n., 86
Bentham, Jeremy, 10
Bentley, Richard, 79–81, 98f.
Bewick, William, 50n.
Bible, The, 111, 138
Bird, Edward, "The Game of Put," 92n.
Blackwood, Captain Price, 42n.
*Blackwood's Magazine,* 8n.
Blessington, Countess of, xi
Blücher, Prince Gebhard von, 53, 66
Boatswain, Byron's dog, 115
Boccaccio, Giovanni, 145, 146n.
Bordeaux, 43
Boswell, James, 111
Bourrienne, Louis, *Mémoires,* 54–56, 72
Boyd, Hugh Stuart, x, 12n., 37n.
Boyd-Carpenter, V., xviii
Boydel Shakespeare Gallery, 21n.
Brigham, Nicholas, 32, 34n.
British Gallery, 116, 170
British Institution, 24, 25n., 28, 29n., 38n.
Brougham, Henry Peter, 66, 67n., 135, 136n.
Brown, John, 111, 112n.
Browning, Elizabeth Barrett (Mrs. Robert Browning). *See* Elizabeth Barrett Barrett
Browning, Robert, x, xi, xiv, xv, xvii, 111n.
Browning, Robert Wiedemann Barrett ("Pen," E.B.B.'s son), xvii
Brydges, Sir Samuel Egerton, 44, 45n.
Buckingham Palace, 87

Burdett, 66, 67n.
Burke, Edmund, 180n.
Byron, Allegra, 114, 117n.
Byron, Annabella, Baroness, 59, 69, 70n., 73–75
Byron, sixth Baron, 16, 74, 75n., 87, 114, 117n., 118, 148; *Don Juan,* 75n.; "Euthanasia," 166, 167n.; "Fare Thee Well," 41, 42n., 64, 66n.

Cacciatore, Vera, xviii
Canace, 33n.
Cannes, 51, 52n.
Carleroi, 54
Carlyle, Thomas, *Past and Present,* 89, 91n.
Carnack, Colonel, 98
Carter, J. H., 19n.
Carter, Matilda, 18, 19n.
Castlereagh, Viscount, 58, 61n., 140n.
Cennini, Cennino, 76
Chalon, Alfred Edward, 125, 126n.
Champs Elysées, 64
Chateauvieux, J. F. Lullin de, *Manuscrit venu de St. Hélène,* 51f.
Chaucer, Geoffrey, xvi, 36; *Troilus and Criseyde,* 33n.; age of, 30, 34n., 43f.; description of self, 33; in B.R.H.'s "Black Prince," xvi, 28f.; opinion of Gower, 32
Chaumont, 64
Chaworth, Mary, 74
Chiswick, 4n.
*Civil Engineer and Architect's Journal, The,* 132, 133n.
Clairmont, Claire, 117n.
Claxton, Marshall, 128; "Alfred in the Danish Camp," 122
Cleopatra, 144
Cobley, Harriet, 65n.
Cockburn, Sir George, 142
Colburn, Henry, 81, 84n.
*Colburn's United Service Magazine,* 51, 52n., 175
Coleridge, Samuel Taylor, xi, 42n., 160
Columbus, Christopher, 100, 101n.
Colville, General Sir Charles, 73, 75n.
Colvin, Sir Sidney, *John Keats,* xvii, 17n.

Grantley, third Baron, 42n.
Greenhithe, 146
Grey, second Earl, xiii
Grignan, Mme. de, 101n.
Grinke, Paul, 180n.
Grouchy, Emmanuel de, 53
Guedalla, Philip, *The Duke*, 169n.
Gurwood, Colonel John, 67n.
Gwatkin, Theophila, 180n.

Hall, Basil, *Napoleon in Council*, 174
Hall, Samuel Carter, 83, 84n.
Hall, Mrs. Samuel Carter, 78, 80n., 82f.
Halle, 53
Hamilton, William, *Aegyptiaca*, 79, 80n.
Hampstead, 16
Harrow-on-the-Hill, 98, 114, 117n.
Hart, Solomon Alexander, 125, 126n.
Haviland, James, 99n.
Haydon, Benjamin Robert (B.R.H.'s father), xii, 76, 112
Haydon, Benjamin Robert
— paintings of: "Adam and Eve," 3, 4n., 8, 35, 48f., 103, 130, 171n.; "Alexander's Combat with the Lion," 11, 12n., 18, 46, 47n., 48n., 65, 79f., 83, 92, 94, 98, 118, 125, 131, 134, 141f., 153f., 164, 166, 167n., 169f.; "The Anti-Slavery Convention," xiii, 66, 67n., 75n., 154n.; "The Assassination of Dentatus," xiii, 24, 46, 86, 87n., 96, 97n.; "The Banishment of Aristides," 182; "The Black Prince Entering London in Triumph," xvi, 11, 12n., 26, 30, 41, 47–49, 103, 126, 127n., 135; "Byron Musing on a Distant View of Harrow," 114, 117n.; "Cassandra," 41, 42n., 167n.; "C'est Lui," 37–40; "Christ's Entry into Jerusalem," xi, xiii, 16, 17n., 46, 47n.; "The Crucifixion," 143, 145; "Curtius Leaping into the Gulf," 11, 13f., 17, 19n., 28, 35, 38n., 40n., 46, 47n., 71, 72n., 85, 97, 116, 166, 170; "The First Child," 94, 163; "George IV and Wellington Visiting Waterloo," 168, 169n., 171f.; "The Judgment of Solomon," xiii, 24, 46, 49, 50n., 73n., 87, 91, 116; "Macbeth," 168, 171f.; "The Maid of Saragossa," 64, 66n., 95–97, 169f.; "The Mock Election," 185; "Napoleon Musing," 17–19, 63, 66n., 152n., 164–166, 169f., 172–174; "Nelson Sealing the Letter at Copenhagen," 125, 141; "Punch," 185; "The Raising of Lazarus," xiii, 98, 99n.; "The Reform Banquet," xiii, 66, 67n., 154n.; "The Spanish Nun," 167n.; "Uriel Revealing himself to Satan," 1, 2n., 152, 176, 183; "Venus and Anchises," 37f., 40n., 57, 58n., "Wellington Musing on the Field of Waterloo," 159n., 174; "William Wordsworth," 163; "Wordsworth on Helvellyn," 2f., 14, 50, 67f., 70n., 159.
— publications of: *Autobiography and Memoirs*, xx, 21n., 22n., 25n., 27n., 78n., 95, 98–100, 103f., 106, 108, 113n., 157n.; "Battle of Waterloo," 175; "The Cartoons," 132, 133n.; *Correspondence and Table-Talk*, xx, 2n., 3n., 31n., 34n., 101n., 178n.; *Diary*, xx, 2n., 9n., 12n., 27n., 48n., 50n., 54n., 61n., 67n., 92n., 93n., 95n., 97n., 103n., 107n., 109n., 111n., 119n., 120n., 136n., 140n., 146n., 150n., 157n., 159n., 186n.; *The Judgment of Connoisseurs*, 135, 136n.; *Life of Wilkie* (review), 132; *Painting and the Fine Arts*, 110, 111n.; *Thoughts on the Relative Value of Fresco and Oil Painting*, 1, 2n.
— argument with E.B.B. on mesmerism, xvi, xvii, 157f.; argument with E.B.B. on Wellington and Napoleon, xvi, xvii, 50f., 54f., 58–60, 62f., 66, 68, 73, 175; attachment to the aristocracy, 167; birthday of, 168; burns foot, 102f., 108, 110; controversy with Beaumont over "Macbeth,"

Wilkie, Helen, 77, 98, 99n., 100
Wilson, John, 7, 8n.
Windsor Castle, 139f.
Winstanley, William, *The Lives of the Most Famous English Poets*, 31, 33n.
Wordsworth, William, xi, xv, 10, 17n., 33, 38n., 68, 87, 100, 129; "Composed upon Westminster Bridge," 36, 37n.; "Grace Darling," 74f.; "I Wandered Lonely as a Cloud," 101n.; *The Letters of William and Dorothy Wordsworth*, 7n., 75n.; "Personal Talk," 5n.; "To B. R. Haydon," 63, 66n.; becomes poet laureate, 69, 74f., 80; friendship with B.R.H., xii, 177; meeting with E.B.B., 3, 4n.; on Helvellyn, 4, 147; writes to E.B.B., 6, 7n.
Wurmser, Dagobert von, 52

Xerxes, 57n.

*Zoist*, 159n.